THE
ARCHANGEL GUIDE TO
ASCENSION

THE
ARCHANGEL GUIDE TO
ASCENSION

55 Steps to the Light

DIANA COOPER AND **TIM WHILD**

HAY HOUSE

Carlsbad, California • New York City • London • Sydney
Johannesburg • Vancouver • Hong Kong • New Delhi

First published and distributed in the United Kingdom by:
Hay House UK Ltd, Astley House, 33 Notting Hill Gate, London W11 3JQ
Tel: +44 (0)20 3675 2450; Fax: +44 (0)20 3675 2451; www.hayhouse.co.uk

Published and distributed in the United States of America by:
Hay House Inc., PO Box 5100, Carlsbad, CA 92018-5100
Tel: (1) 760 431 7695 or (800) 654 5126
Fax: (1) 760 431 6948 or (800) 650 5115; www.hayhouse.com

Published and distributed in Australia by:
Hay House Australia Ltd, 18/36 Ralph St, Alexandria NSW 2015
info@hayhouse.co.za; www.hayhouse.com.au

Published and distributed in the Republic of South Africa by:
Hay House SA (Pty) Ltd, PO Box 990, Witkoppen 2068
Tel/Fax: (27) 11 467 8904; www.hayhouse.co.za

Published and distributed in India by:
Hay House Publishers India, Muskaan Complex, Plot No.3, B-2,
Vasant Kunj, New Delhi 110 070
Tel: (91) 11 4176 1620; Fax: (91) 11 4176 1630; www.hayhouse.co.in

Distributed in Canada by:
Raincoast Books, 2440 Viking Way, Richmond, B.C. V6V 1N2
Tel: (1) 604 448 7100; Fax: (1) 604 270 7161; www.raincoast.com

A catalogue record for this book is available from the British Library.

ISBN: 978-1-78180-471-1

Printed and bound in Great Britain by TJ International Ltd, Padstow, Cornwall

Contents

Introduction

Meeting Tim

This is such a high-frequency book that I want to start by sharing what happened at my pre-life consultation for this life. I was called to a meeting with my guide, Kumeka, my guardian angel and Archangel Metatron. No one else was present.

I was asked to undertake a mission on Earth. I was shown my parents and family and was told that I would have to incarnate immediately. There was no time for discussion or consideration. My options were to accept or decline! As I'm here, obviously I accepted.

I was born in 1940 in the Himalayas at the exact moment the first bomb fell on London. My task was to act as a light to counteract the darkness.

I went through the Veil of Amnesia and forgot my divine connections, but when the travails of life became too much for me, the angels dragged me into the light again and I have worked with them ever since. This is the 27th book I have written with Kumeka and the angels.

I met Tim when he came to a book-signing in a store. As I wrote in his copy of my book, *Discover Atlantis*, I asked him what he did for a living. He was a gardener and I needed one.

Later, when I asked him to cut down a scruffy hawthorn tree at the end of my garden, he came in to tell me the hawthorn said it was protecting me and my home. I thought, *Who is this man?*

Over a cup of tea he shared his desire to become an ascension teacher. I told him to pick up his book and reread it. As we talked, little white feathers started to pour over us. When he left, I counted more than 400 feathers laid out in small squares over the entire lawn.

He phoned me from his holiday to say he had read the book and knew exactly who he had been in Atlantis and why he was here now.

Years passed and he came back to do some gardening. A mutual friend happened to be in the kitchen at the time and said, 'Do you realize when Tim walked in all your 12 chakras lit up?'

Ah, I thought. *He is ready for his mission.*

Diana

Meeting Diana

I was born in southern England in 1972 and have been spiritually connected since I can remember. Running a high frequency in the older, denser vibrations was very challenging for me as a child.

My life changed completely in 1990 after an accident and I started to study the spiritual works of authors around the planet.

Over the period of my awakening, I discovered that I was the physical aspect of Thoth, high priest of Atlantis. From this point onwards, I fully committed myself to the progress and ascension of planet Earth and all who live upon her.

I met Diana at a local book-signing in Bournemouth, UK. She had just released *Discover Atlantis*. Later I realized we had worked closely together in the era of Atlantis. The universe had decided that it was time for us to work together again and I started helping her in her garden. We live close to each other.

As the years passed, our friendship blossomed and we have supported each other through the many life changes we have been through.

We work fantastically together and last year Archangel Metatron, who is in charge of the entire ascension process of this universe, announced that we were to produce new cutting-edge ascension information to assist with the planetary changes.

So we have created this book for you. It is a powerful seventh-dimensional co-operation that will illuminate all who read it.

Tim

Steps to Ascension

We are now in a transitional period to a new Golden Age. This transition started at the Cosmic Moment, 21 December 2012, which was the end of the 260,000-year-long Atlantis experiment. The exploration of the third dimension which started with the setting up of Atlantis is now being wound down to make way for an entirely new reality.

The last 10,000 years of the Atlantis experiment have been third-dimensional, but in 2014 the planet moved into the fourth dimension. We are now part of a brand new planetary and cosmic dynamic. This is bringing a completely new frequency into the lives of every sentient being on the planet.

Archangels are stepping in now to help us all to raise our frequency to the fifth dimension and beyond. Archangel Metatron, who vibrates with the number 55, has asked us to present you with 55 steps to ascension so that you can raise your frequency quickly and, in turn, help others to ascend. He is overlighting this book. To overlight is to oversee, almost as a project manager would. So Metatron will be with you as you work with the guidance.

Archangels are not the only Illumined Beings who are helping with our glorious ascension process. Unicorns, the purest of the pure, are shimmering white horses who have ascended into the seventh to ninth dimensions of the angelic realms and they assist our journey by touching those who are ready with their radiant horn of spiralling light.

Many elementals, from the fifth-dimensional goblins and fairies to the negativity-consuming esaks of the third dimension, are helping us to become a glowing golden planet. Those beautiful fourth-dimensional elementals the dragons are waiting to be our faithful friends and companions and to serve us in a number of ways. For the first time, teams of fifth-dimensional golden dragons are here to assist and protect us. We are living in wonderful times and are incredibly loved, protected and assisted by the angelic realms.

We have been asked to create this book together to offer a perfect balance of masculine and feminine energy. Each step offers guidance about the archangels, information about the step itself and a visualization or other exercise to help you. The steps are sequential so that as you absorb the information of each one you can move easily to the following one. You will be helped to ascend by an archangelic current flowing through the book, so we are taking you on a very exciting journey. We literally buzzed with energy as we received the information.

It is enlightening to start by reconnecting with the invitation you were given by Lady Gaia to incarnate on Earth. Lady Gaia is the Throne who is in charge of our planet. Thrones are ninth-dimensional angels who look after the stars and planets, and Lady Gaia literally ensouls Earth. Remembering her invitation to incarnate here enables you to remember your soul contract, and this is the first step of the journey Archangel Metatron wishes to present.

The most important foundations for living in ascended frequencies are to meet the elemental dragons who will transmute lower frequencies, then to immerse yourself in Archangel Metatron's energy to empower your journey. This will enable you to anchor your 12 fifth-dimensional chakras – spiritual energy centres that hold light and wisdom. You will also be able to activate your fifth-dimensional merkabah, the energetic six-pointed star that surrounds your aura and contains your fifth-dimensional blueprint.

We offer many tools, attunements, visualizations and archangelic connections to accelerate your ascension to the upper levels of the fifth dimension. We believe these will be of great assistance to you on your spiritual path.

Step 1

Lady Gaia and Your Soul Contract

B efore we incarnate our soul attends a special meeting on the inner planes. Our guardian angel, who has been with us throughout our soul journey, including our visits to Earth, is always present. So is our overlighting archangel, to whom feedback is passed every seven years about how we are progressing on our journey until we reach the fifth dimension. After that, the archangel monitors us constantly. (Most of us are overlit by Archangels Metatron, Michael, Gabriel, Raphael or Uriel, but occasionally a different archangel works with a person. Some children are coming in now with a very high vibration and because of this higher frequency, other archangels, and even Seraphina, one of the 12th-dimensional Seraphim, are overlighting them.)

Our principal guide and sometimes other guides and masters also attend this important gathering. Usually other angels are there, too, as well as members of the extended family we are about to join, including our future children. We have often seen Orbs of angels bringing souls to have a look at their possible family before they attend the pre-life meeting and make their commitment.

During this pre-life consultation we discuss with all these beings what we want to experience in this life or to offer to others. Some very brave souls step forward to enable others, usually in their soul group, to learn about unconditional love, compassion, patience, faith, grace or other ascension qualities.

For this, we or the other soul may agree to experience disability, mental challenges, accidents, illness or some of the more difficult tests. In our current times an easy life does not offer growth, so a challenging path is more desirable to souls who really want to progress to ascension. We may also want to burn off family, ancestral or country karma, for it is time for us all to step off the wheel of karma.

After our pre-life meeting and before we incarnate, Lady Gaia issues us with an invitation to take a physical body here on Earth. This invitation is given to us directly from her radiant heart with enormous love and the warmest welcome. Its purpose is to enable us to feel that we belong on Earth – and it is placed in our own open heart.

When we truly remember this invitation and the glowing unconditional love with which Lady Gaia has issued it to us, we feel comfortable and at home wherever we are and whoever we are with. We feel we truly belong.

Because so many of us have lost this connection, however, Lady Gaia has asked us to present you with this meditation.

Visualization to Remember Your Pre-Life Decisions

1. Prepare a space where you can be relaxed and undisturbed. Light a candle if you can to raise the energy.

2. Sit quietly and breathe comfortably with the intention of remembering your pre-life decisions.

3. Ground yourself by visualizing roots going from your feet deep into the Earth.

4. Ask Archangel Michael to place his deep blue cloak of protection around you.

5. Call in your pure white unicorn and allow it to shower you with blessings. Ask it to take you to the Temple of Light. The Temple of Light is one of the many inner and higher-plane retreats. A retreat is a focal point of the

energy of an archangel or master.

6. Feel yourself rising on your unicorn through the dimensions until you see the Temple of Light ahead, shimmering with blue-green radiance.

7. Your unicorn flies with you to the central courtyard, where it lands and you dismount.

8. Your guardian angel steps into the courtyard to greet you and enfold you in love. Relax into this embrace.

9. Your guardian angel takes you into a chamber that is lit up with the colour of your overlighting archangel. Is it Archangel Metatron's golden orange? Archangel Michael's deep blue? Archangel Gabriel's pure white? Archangel Raphael's emerald green or Archangel Uriel's golden yellow?

10. Your overlighting archangel steps forward to greet you. Sense their light enfolding you in unconditional acceptance and love.

11. Your guide (or guides) now welcomes you. Have a sense of their wisdom, love and dedication to you.

12. You see the light-filled Higher Selves of your entire family.

13. Take your time to consult all these beings and understand why your life decisions were made.

14. Thank them all for coming.

15. Ask Archangel Sandalphon to ground you in Earth's energy and gently return to where you started.

Meeting Lady Gaia

1. Climb onto your magnificent unicorn and let it carry you down a shaft of pure white light into Hollow Earth, the vast seventh-dimensional chakra in the centre of Earth where every being, every civilization or culture that has ever incarnated is represented in etheric form.

2. Your unicorn glides with you through this wonderland and you can see magnificent dragons, people from ancient cultures, animals and many beings of light.

3. In the very centre of Hollow Earth is a vast shimmering crystal pyramid. Step off your unicorn and enter it.

4. Here waiting for you is Lady Gaia, a huge, wondrous blue-green angel.

5. She opens her heart, which radiates pink light, and gives you a warm smile of welcome.

6. She reminds you how much she loves you and wants you on Earth.

7. She places her hand on your heart and you may feel it buzz or glow. Then she places your original invitation to Earth into it.

8. She reactivates it with a special high-frequency humming sound.

9. Know you belong. Feel it in your heart.

10. Remain with Lady Gaia as long as you need to.

11. Thank her.

12. Return to your unicorn, who takes you back through Hollow Earth to the place where you started.

Step 2

The Unicorns

One of the greatest ascension gifts we can receive in this lifetime is to connect to our unicorn. In the Golden Era of Atlantis everyone had their own unicorn and they were able to communicate with them, just as they did with their guardian angels. However, as Atlantis devolved, the unicorns could not cope with the lower frequency, so they withdrew. Now at last enough of us have raised our vibration for the unicorns to return.

Unicorns are seventh- to ninth-dimensional beings who belong to the seventh heaven. Glorious seventh-dimensional unicorns started to return to Earth when people's lights started to go on. Since 2012 wondrous ninth-dimensional unicorns, breathtaking in the intensity of their radiance, have started to pour light onto individuals and the planet. Unlike angels, they have experienced a physical body, for they are pure white horses who have undertaken all their lessons on Earth and have become perfected beings and ascended in a glorious burst of light. In their spiritual bodies as unicorns, they work with us at a soul level.

Unicorns are fully enlightened, so spiralling white energy radiates from their third eye chakra and this is seen as their horn of light. Their light is so powerful that we can only accept a little at a time. The unicorns ensure that we receive what we are ready for.

When we connect with these pure light beings, they greatly assist our path of enlightenment and ascension. They are actively looking for people who radiate a light and aspire to help others and the world.

They help in a number of ways:

- When we have a vision, they help us to hold onto it by giving us the qualities, such as faith, strength and personal magnetism, that we need to bring it to fruition.

- They also facilitate the desires of our soul by taking them to Source – the Creator, God. This helps us fulfil our pre-life contract and sometimes enables great visions to be fulfilled.

- Through their horn of light they direct physical, mental, emotional and soul healing to us. Remember to ask for it.

- They also help heal and clear deep karmic wounds. These can be personal or connected with our family or country.

- We can ask them to balance and align our 12 fifth-dimensional chakras while we sleep.

Unicorns also help to reconnect us to our spirit. When part of our essence has withdrawn due to illness or trauma, we can ask them to make us whole again. This is especially beneficial for high-frequency children who find it difficult to ground their energies on Earth. Unicorns touch and help all children, but especially those who are very pure and innocent.

Just thinking about a unicorn aligns us to their energy and the higher spiritual realms. They take us into the seventh dimension, where they help us to develop the qualities they possess – love, peace, calmness, gentleness, hope, majesty, caring, wisdom, compassion, magic and mystery.

We are now going to help you enter a meditative space where you can meet your unicorn or make a deeper connection with it and receive healing, karmic clearance, enlightenment and assistance on your ascension path. Your unicorn will also take you to Source for divine blessing on your soul mission.

A Visualization to Work with Unicorns

If you simply read this exercise it is very effective. If you close your eyes and enter a meditative state, it can really enable the unicorns to touch your essence.

1. Prepare a space where you can be relaxed and undisturbed. Light a candle if you can.

2. Sit quietly and breathe comfortably with the intention of surrendering to unicorn energy.

3. Ground yourself by visualizing roots going from your feet deep into the Earth.

4. Ask Archangel Michael to place his deep blue cloak of protection around you.

5. Surround yourself with a ball of pure white light. Gently and slowly breathe in this light and feel it relaxing your body. Imagine the pure white light soothing you as it flows gently through your body.

6. Mentally call in your unicorn. And now sense or see a magnificent shimmering white horse approaching you. It is peaceful and harmless and gentle and you feel enfolded in love as it approaches.

7. As your beautiful unicorn stands quietly by you, ask it to balance and light up your 12 fifth-dimensional chakras. See the pure white light flowing down through your Stellar Gateway, 15 inches (45 centimetres) above your head, your soul star, 7 inches (18 centimetres) below that, your causal chakra, offset to the back of your crown, and then down through your crown, third eye, throat, heart, solar plexus, navel, sacral and base chakras and into your Earth Star chakra, 12 inches (30 centimetres) beneath your feet.

8. Visualize a rod of pure white light coming from your Monad, your soul group, through to Hollow Earth.

9. Thank your unicorn.

Unicorn Healing and Release of Karmic Wounds

1. Connect to your unicorn.

2. Ask it, either mentally or out loud, to give you the healing you need:

   'Beloved Unicorn, I ask you to pour your light into me, healing me physically, emotionally, mentally and at a deep soul level. I am ready to receive.'

3. Your unicorn bends its head and touches your heart with its horn of light. Seventh-dimensional energy is now pouring through your physical, emotional and mental body. It is touching your soul. Breathe in the shimmering white light and feel it flowing through you. Your fifth-dimensional merkabah, the six-pointed star surrounding your aura, is lighting up around you.

4. Ask your unicorn to heal any karmic wounds you may have from this or any other life:

   'Beloved Unicorn, I pray for the healing of any karmic wounds I may carry consciously or unconsciously. It is done.'

5. Feel the shower of light streaming over and through you.

6. Ask your unicorn to heal any family karmic wounds you may have from this or any other life:

   'Beloved Unicorn, I pray for the healing of any karmic wounds within my family that we may carry consciously or unconsciously. It is done.'

7. Feel the shower of light streaming over and through you and your family, including your ancestors.

8. Ask your unicorn to heal any karmic wounds that your country may hold from recent times or ancient history:

   'Beloved Unicorn, I pray for the healing of any karmic wounds within my country. It is done.'

9. Visualize the shower of light streaming over and through your entire country, deep into the land itself.

10. Thank your unicorn for all you have received.

Unicorns Reconnect Your Spirit or Soul

1. Connect to your unicorn.

2. Ask it to reconnect any aspect of your spirit or soul that may have withdrawn. Wait while this is completed.

3. Focus on children or adults who are ungrounded or autistic and ask the unicorns to reconnect any aspect of their spirit or soul that may find it difficult to be fully present on Earth.

4. Ask the unicorns to bestow upon humanity an ascension blessing and acceleration.

5. Thank the unicorns for the grace they have bestowed upon you and on others through your intercession.

Unicorns Energize Your Soul Mission

1. Connect to your unicorn.

2. Contemplate your ambitions or expectations. Ask your unicorn to confer on you the qualities you need to bring these plans to fruition.

3. Ask your unicorn to open your consciousness fully to your soul mission. Ask it to grant you the qualities you need to bring this to fruition.

4. Your beautiful unicorn has been pouring light into you. Now it is inviting you to climb onto its back so that it can take you and your vision and/or soul mission to Source for a blessing.

5. You find yourself lightly and easily leaping onto its back. You feel so safe and comfortable, as if you belong here.

6. Feeling totally secure on your unicorn, be aware that it is rising into the air and gently gliding above the treetops. You see all of nature spread out below you as you move higher and higher.

7. Ahead there is a brilliant rainbow arching across the sky, promising hope, and you find yourself moving through the colours into different dimensions.

8. Vast angelic beings surround you and celebrate your journey into the higher realms. Many unicorns glide in front of you and others follow you. You are in the centre of a procession of light beings moving through the seventh heaven and even higher.

9. Steps appear before you, shimmering and sparkling like diamonds. You ride your unicorn up them. Magnificent Seraphim surround you. These mighty angels are taking you into the glorious light of Source.

10. Whether you are aware of it or not, you are receiving a special blessing from Source to energize your soul mission on Earth. Rest in this ineffable light. Every cell and fibre of your being is being touched by Source. Your body is becoming a trillion pinpricks of light.

11. Know that you are a beloved child of God. Feel this deep inside. New doors are opening. The universe is waiting for you with bated breath. You are wearing a mantle of pure light.

12. Your unicorn is gradually moving away from this wondrous light, withdrawing you slowly from this incredible holy space.

13. It is carrying you down the diamond steps and back down through the vast universe.

14. It is bearing you through the rainbow and into the angelic and unicorn kingdom.

15. Here the angels and unicorns are smiling at you and stroking your shimmering aura. They see your huge potential and possibilities, brought forward by your journey with your unicorn to Source.

16. They too are blessing you, adding thousands of blessings to those you have received from Source.

17. Consciously or unconsciously, you see everything and everyone from a higher, wider cosmic perspective. Your levels of enlightenment have expanded. Your light levels have risen hugely.

18. Your unicorn is gently carrying you down through the stars until you can see the blue-green light of Earth below you.

19. On your unicorn you are landing, smooth as a whisper, on the ground.

20. Thank your unicorn for all it has done to help you. Know that you can invoke it at any time.

21. Now it is time to pull your aura in again. Stretch and smile. The unicorns are with you.

You can read the above or do it as a visualization as often as you wish. Be aware it is a powerful ascension accelerator and you may need to rest afterwards.

Step 3

Prepare Your 12 Chakras and Activate Your Fifth-Dimensional Merkabah

During the Golden Age of Atlantis everyone had 12 chakras in place which contained the codes of all their extraordinary gifts and talents. As the energy devolved, five chakras were switched off.

At the same time the fifth-dimensional merkabah dissolved. This was the energetic six-pointed star that surrounded our aura and contained our fifth-dimensional blueprint and light body. (Our light body holds all the light and wisdom codes we have earned in the course of our soul journey. It is the physical manifestation of our Higher Self.) The fifth-dimensional merkabah was replaced by the third-dimensional merkabah so that the remaining seven chakras radiated at a lower frequency.

It is now time for us all to bring back our 12 chakras and our whole range of extraordinary gifts and talents. Then we can bring in a new civilization and a new Golden Age on the planet. This will have the imprint of Golden Ascended Atlantis, but our task is to recreate it at an even higher frequency.

We can reinstate our fifth-dimensional chakras ourselves, and when they are installed and operational, our fifth-dimensional merkabah will automatically be anchored.

Note that we are now moving metaphorically from a house with five floors to a skyscraper with 12 floors. Therefore our foundation, which in the 12-chakra system is our Earth Star chakra, needs to be much stronger than before and fully anchored. This is our connection, our roots, into Gaia. Archangel Sandalphon anchors these roots for us when we are ready.

What is currently happening is that many evolved people are bringing in their fifth-dimensional chakras and are finding it easy to open their higher chakras: the crown, third eye, throat, heart and solar plexus. However, as the higher energy comes down, it is getting stuck in the sacral and base chakras. This is because there are still many lessons for us all to learn about basic survival and relationship issues. Survival and emotional fears, which are held in the lower chakras, are keeping the base and sacral chakras third-dimensional. So the lessons involved keep being re-presented, as they have to be learned right now.

If you are reading this book, it suggests you are being fast-tracked, so the archangels will present you with opportunities to learn these lessons. So, look at the challenges being offered to you, learn from them and follow the simple exercise below to bring in your fifth-dimensional sacral and base chakras.

We are offering you this exercise to prepare all your 12 chakras and anchor your fifth-dimensional merkabah. This will enable you to move into a magnificent future as a light being.

Prepare and Activate Your 12 Chakras

You may need to do this meditation daily for some time or you may find that weekly or even monthly is perfect for your level of development. Use your discernment. It will eventually enable you to live permanently in the fifth dimension, which is most important for your ascension and that of the planet.

You may like to practise this as a formal meditation to start with, but when you know it, you will be able to do it while walking, gardening, doing housework, sitting on public transport or whenever you have a quiet moment. All invocations can be used silently (mentally), particularly when on a bus. If you need to be reminded of what to do, you can always carry this book with you or note down the information on a piece of paper.

1. First make a sacred space. Sacred space can be anywhere quiet or private. Sit comfortably. Light a candle if possible and relax.

2. Call in Archangel Michael to protect your space and clear any lower frequencies from around you.

3. Invite the fire dragons to place a wall of fire round you and burn up any residue that Archangel Michael cannot reach.

4. Invite Archangel Metatron to run a column of high-frequency golden orange ascension light down from your Monad to your Earth Star. This will also ground you.

5. Visualize the column of glowing light opening all your existing chakras completely and clearing any remaining debris.

6. Ask Archangel Metatron to touch, light up and fully activate your Stellar Gateway, which is the gateway to all your monadic wisdom. It is about 15 inches (45 centimetres) above your head. See it as your own personal golden orange Sun above you.

7. Visualize a bridge of light between yourself and Source. This is your Antakarana bridge – an Indian term describing a bridge of light between soul and vessel. Visualize your bridge starting to energize and shine.

8. Ask Archangel Mariel to touch, light up and fully activate the higher aspect of your soul star chakra, which is 7 inches (18 centimetres) below the Stellar Gateway and is a glorious magenta pink. It contains all your soul's incredible knowledge and wisdom and you can use this to activate your own personal skills and powers as a master. Take a few moments to visualize yourself using the skills you had in Golden Ascended Atlantis for your highest good.

9. Ask Archangel Christiel to touch, light up and fully activate your causal chakra, above and slightly behind your crown chakra, so that it is a glorious glowing pure white. This is where you connect with the spiritual world, the angelic frequencies and the unicorns. Here you access the secrets of deep peace and eternal life.

10. Ask Archangel Jophiel to touch, light up and fully activate your crown chakra, which is the thousand-petalled lotus at the top of your head. This opens when you are ready to accept the codes of higher light and Source wisdom. You can ask the unicorns to help you open the petals. Visualize Archangel Jophiel pouring the golden-white light of wisdom through this chakra into every facet of your being.

11. Ask Archangel Raphael to touch, light up and fully activate the crystal ball which is your fifth-dimensional third eye. See it as totally clear, enabling you to see through all the Veils and dimensions. When you focus your thoughts, you truly become a co-creator with the divine. Now use the power of your third eye to co-create an abundance of all things by visualizing it. Send healing with the focus of the mind by picturing divine perfection in all things.

12. Ask Archangel Michael to touch, light up and fully activate your royal blue fifth-dimensional throat chakra. Archangel Michael will assist you to speak the languages of light and truth. Now communicate with the masters and angels on the golden ray. This is another facet of the many high-frequency light sources that are available. It is of a very high vibration and invoked in the same manner as any other spiritual energy.

13. Ask Archangel Chamuel to touch, light up and fully activate the 33 petals of your heart until you hold a pure white rose with touches of soft pink in your heart chakra. You are now connected through Venus to the ninth-dimensional aspect of the Cosmic Heart. This is the source of pure love that is channelled into usable facets by the higher realms. Be aware of Archangel Mary, the universal angel, flooding your heart with love, compassion and healing.

14. Ask Archangel Uriel to touch, light up and fully activate the ball of golden knowledge and wisdom that is your solar plexus chakra. Bring through your soul knowledge and all the knowledge of the Earth, so that you feel a golden cosmic glow here. You are united with all the wisdom you have accumulated on your soul journey. You are in alignment and trust with the universe. Relax and experience this.

15. Ask Archangel Gabriel to touch, light up and fully activate your welcoming radiant orange navel chakra. Sense your boundaries dissolving as your whole world becomes a family of light within a community of love. See

yourself opening your arms to embrace all people of all cultures and creeds. Experience oneness.

16. Ask Archangel Gabriel to touch, light up and fully activate your iridescent pink sacral chakra, flooding it with transcendent love and harmony. Visualize all your cords with others dissolving and your relationships free and happy. You are now free to experience the flow of higher love.

17. Ask Archangel Gabriel to touch, light up and fully activate your sparkling platinum base chakra so that your life is founded in trust that the universe will provide for your needs. See yourself relaxing into your role as a fifth-dimensional master. You command all your needs from the universe and live in sheer bliss.

18. Ask Archangel Sandalphon to touch, light up and fully activate your black-and-white or haematite-grey Earth Star chakra, which is 12 inches (30 centimetres) below your feet. This is your personal Garden of Eden and the seeds of your vast potential are held here. Take a few moments to visualize Archangel Sandalphon helping you to water and nurture the flourishing garden of who you truly can be. Your Earth Star is your connection to Hollow Earth, the seventh-dimensional chakra in the centre of the planet, where Lady Gaia resides. Sense filaments of light connecting you deep into Mother Earth. Have a sense of being loved and welcomed on Earth and truly belonging here.

19. Invoke Archangel Metatron now to pour down a pillar of golden orange ascension light. Visualize it as a radiant beam pouring down from your Monad, through your Stellar Gateway right down through into Hollow Earth.

20. Invoke Archangel Sandalphon to anchor the beam into Gaia.

21. Archangel Metatron is now holding the construction and energy of your fifth-dimensional merkabah. Visualize him placing your merkabah in the form of two interlinked pyramids of light, forming a six-pointed star, over you.

22. Feel yourself expanding into your fifth-dimensional blueprint and light body. Breathe deeply and slowly as you integrate this energy. Feel every in-breath as pure Source energy and every out-breath as pure light.

23. Give yourself time to relax and absorb this into every cell of your body and spread into your aura.

24. To finish, call on Archangel Michael to surround you in his deep blue protective energy and ensure you are fully grounded into your new body.

25. Open your eyes and smile. At this moment you are a fifth-dimensional master.

Step 4

Archangel Metatron

The mighty Archangel Metatron is the creator of all known light in our universe. Light contains information and knowledge, and Metatron's energy spreads throughout all the universes, encompassing all the dimensional realities right up to the twelfth.

This huge, divine Illumined Being is vast beyond our comprehension and enters our sphere of existence via Helios, the Great Central Sun, the divine core of our entire universe. It is in Helios that Metatron creates the light matter that is the foundation of our existence. The various dimensions that we occupy as physical beings are constructed by light vibrating at different speeds and geometric frequencies. Sacred geometry is used to bind this all together and this lowers the frequency, creating the solid world that we see, touch and sense around us.

As well as having this awesome role of creating matter, Archangel Metatron is responsible for spearheading the ascension process here on Earth.

Energetically, he is predominantly masculine and is often perceived as a vast golden orange Sun exuding power and divine strength.

On Earth, Archangel Metatron's angelic retreat is above Luxor in Egypt. He also holds a vast pool of ascension energy in the etheric (the ethers beyond the physical plane) above the Great Pyramid of Giza. This is distributed in harmony with universal flow to assist Earth and the people living on it in order to accelerate their ascension process.

Due to the tireless work of Archangel Metatron and the myriad of other Illumined Beings helping him, the ascension process is now fully under way. Most lightworkers actively helping the ascension of Earth are attuned to Metatron's energy and guidance. He can co-ordinate thousands of souls at the same time and particularly excels at bringing groups of lightworkers together to achieve a result to benefit humanity.

Archangel Metatron has been present throughout the annals of written and unwritten history. He watched the birth of our world and he has nurtured and guided it throughout the highs and lows that have accompanied us on our journey to this moment in time. Ancient civilizations and all of our modern-day religions contain references to and records of this magnificent archangel.

Atlantis, the first great experiment in which humans took a physical body, was overseen by a host of Divine Beings guided by the power of Archangel Metatron. In the era of Golden Atlantis everyone had 12 strands of DNA fully active and these contained their extraordinary gifts and powers. At the fall of Atlantis, this was reduced to two.

Following the fall, Metatron worked in harmony with the high priests and priestesses of Atlantis who took their tribes to other parts of the world. In Egypt he particularly overlit the ascended master Serapis Bey, widely known as the Egyptian. The ancient Egyptians' extensive knowledge of universal light and physics enabled the pyramids to be constructed using sound, gravity and vibrational technology. Six cosmic pyramids were created in this way throughout the world – at a time when humans had been stripped of the god-like abilities and awesome gifts they had possessed in the Golden Era of Atlantis and were being forced to explore third-dimensional reality in depth.

To this day, the light, frequency and spiritual essence of Archangel Metatron exist within the cells and blueprint of every one of us. This means that we can all connect with him whenever we wish. This is one of the fastest and most powerful ways to accelerate our personal ascension path and those of the people around us. When we ask Archangel Metatron to guide us, it opens incredible opportunities for planetary and intergalactic service.

Under his command he also has a legion of angels known as the Light of Metatron. They come from his solar heart and work in all the other universes as well as our own. All these angels are born in the core of Helios, the gateway between our universe and that of the Infinite Creator.

Below are some simple and very effective techniques that will connect you to the incredible energy of Archangel Metatron and raise your levels of light every time you use them.

The Four-Body System Ascension Boost

The four-body system encompasses your physical, emotional, mental and spiritual bodies. The four-body ascension boost is very powerful. It will run a light current through your body that will instigate an ascension process within you. This will be triggered when the light within your cells reaches 80 per cent and upwards. This starts the descent of the fifth-dimensional chakra column, replacing the fourth-dimensional chakras, and the activation of your full 12 strands of DNA.

Your Higher Self is in full command of this process and will never allow you to have more light than will serve you. Nevertheless, we suggest you do not ask for more than 81 per cent of light until you have been doing this exercise safely for at least three weeks.

By undertaking this exercise, you are fully committing to your ascension path.

1. Prepare a space where you can be relaxed and undisturbed.

2. Sit quietly and breathe comfortably with the intention of activating the four-body ascension boost.

3. Ground yourself by visualizing roots going from your feet deep into the Earth.

4. Ask Archangel Michael to place his deep blue cloak of protection around you.

5. Light a candle and dedicate it to the legions of Archangel Metatron.

6. Ask, either aloud or silently, for Archangel Metatron to fill your physical body with 81 per cent of light.

7. Sense your physical body filling with pure golden orange light.

8. Breathe it into every cell of your body.

9. Ask, either aloud or silently, for Archangel Metatron to fill your emotional body with 81 per cent of light.

10. Sense your emotional body aligning with the peace and love of universal flow.

11. Ask, either aloud or silently, for Archangel Metatron to fill your mental body with 81 per cent of light.

12. Sense your thoughts becoming pure and loving and filled with unconditional love.

13. Ask, either aloud or silently, for Archangel Metatron to fill your spiritual body with 81 per cent of light.

14. See your vast spiritual self ascending gloriously into the fifth dimension and glowing like the Sun.

15. Thank Archangel Metatron.

You are now holding the light of an ascended master. You can maintain this frequency through diligence and focus. Once on this path you will be guided by your Higher Self and your life will change for the better.

Being Touched by Archangel Metatron's Solar Angels

1. Prepare for this meditation.

2. Relax and surrender to Archangel Metatron.

3. Ask him to surround you in his glorious golden orange energy and lift you to the heart of the Great Central Sun.

4. Feel yourself merge with the core of Helios.

5. Sense hundreds of Archangel Metatron's angels pouring through your own heart.

6. They surround you and are connected to you, helping you at all times.

7. Every cell of your body is now illuminated with Archangel Metatron's golden orange light.

8. Thank Archangel Metatron.

Archangel Metatron's Light Bath

1. Prepare for meditation.
2. In meditation, ask Archangel Metatron to prepare his light bath for you.
3. As you relax you may be aware of a gentle current of light running through your body.
4. Either aloud or silently, make this invocation:

   'Archangel Metatron, please now place me within your light bath.'

5. All around you in precise geometric locations are pillars of beautiful, golden, glowing light. You are lying at the centre of a spacious Metatron Cube, a sacred geometrical form showing the cosmic connection within this universe.
6. Imagine every cell of your body becoming pure honey-golden liquid light.
7. Feel Archangel Metatron's divine presence as he places his hands upon you. Relax totally as the archangel pours his frequency through every cell of your being.
8. The room is becoming brighter as Archangel Metatron amplifies the light level of the bath to suit your needs precisely.
9. Ask Archangel Metatron to dissolve anything within your body, aura or fields that you know has been an issue during the day.
10. Feel his golden light flowing through every chakra, opening them and spinning them at a fifth-dimensional frequency.
11. Ask Archangel Metatron to hold your perfect level of light within your body and fields at all times, day and night.
12. Thank him.
13. Relax and rest.

Step 5

The Great Central Sun

Our Sun, the beautiful radiance in our sky, provider of nourishment and warmth for life here on Earth, is a star in physical form. Not only this, it is a conscious, evolving super-being with a specific plan to assist the construction and progression of our galactic space.

The recent physical, mental, emotional and spiritual changes in individuals and the planet have been fortified by amazing magnetic radioactive triggers provided at key moments by the Sun. These have coincided with astrological alignments that were predicted very accurately by ancient civilizations who foresaw the coming of the Age of Aquarius.

As our Sun radiates light and beauty upon us, it is fuelled esoterically by another source, a greater provider, the Great Central Sun. This exists beyond the range of our third-dimensional visual reality and is the birthing pool for all cosmic light, wisdom, knowledge and matter in our known and unknown universe. It is currently beyond our ability to understand this concept.

What we do know is that Source is the creative force behind all spiritual matter and the Great Central Sun steps down Source energy at a ninth-dimensional level. Within its light, at a spiritual level, all things are constructed. It gave birth to Metatron and Shekinah, the divine masculine and feminine opposites, mind and birth, that merged together to create physical life on our planet. In the Bible Metatron and Shekinah are referred to as Adam and Eve.

The Great Central Sun encapsulates the energy of the Cosmic Heart and the angelic realm. Most of the extra-terrestrials, higher forces and beings of light that are currently flocking to help us originated here.

Although we cannot perceive the light from the Great Central Sun, we can receive it and can most certainly feel it. It is pouring continual streams of high-frequency God-light onto us all, helping us to blossom into ascended masters.

We are being provided with a series of intensive lessons that are helping us to transcend the current fourth-dimensional reality. It is anticipated that a significant number of people will shift into the fifth dimension in 2015.

As mentioned earlier, the mighty Archangel Metatron is in charge of the universal light distributed from the core of the Great Central Sun. The Great Central Sun gave birth to Orion, which is Archangel Metatron's constellation. It is his true home and his workshop for forging the atomic light structure for every dimension that spirals out to the far reaches of the universe.

We share this great etheric light with our star-seed brothers and sisters from the Pleiades, Andromeda, Sirius, Lyra and the many other stars, planets and galaxies that have contributed genetically to our human blueprint.

As we go through our glorious ascension process, the light from the Great Central Sun, pouring through the portal of our own Sun, is now also becoming the source of body fuel for the higher crystalline light form into which we are moving.

Archangel Metatron would like to take you through a short visualization to introduce you to the direct frequency of the Great Central Sun. He will step down the light, as it is too great for us to cope with in our current form.

Visualization to Connect with the Great Central Sun

During this journey every cell of your body will melt and re-form with the flow surrounding and running through you. You will have the absolute certainty that you are in the arms of your Creator. You may remain cocooned there for as long as you wish, absorbing the frequency.

1. Prepare a space where you can be relaxed and undisturbed. Light a candle if you can.

2. Sit quietly and breathe comfortably with the intention of connecting with the Great Central Sun.

3. Ground yourself by visualizing roots going from your feet deep into the Earth.

4. Ask Archangel Michael to place his deep blue cloak of protection around you.

5. Be aware of a radiant golden light flooding into your aura from above.

6. Slowly you are aware that you are being carried upwards, suspended in a tube of light, accompanied by a radiant angelic figure, a member of the Light of Metatron.

7. You are travelling up through the sky and into space.

8. You start to become aware of a new source of light that is bonding with your atomic structure and vibrating oneness with every cell of your being.

9. You become aware that you are no longer a separate organism. You are the light. The light is you.

10. Your tube of light has also melted and become one with the universal glow around you.

11. Archangel Metatron whispers to you. 'Welcome to the Light of the Great Central Sun, your creator, your essence, your universal core. This is where your spark began. This was the start of your great journey. This is the gateway to the Hand of Source.'

12. Breathe deeply. Absorb the Light.

13.   And take this great Light back to all those with whom you share your life.

When you have returned from your journey, every cell of your body will be glowing with an etheric light – iridescent and stunningly beautiful. This is your gift to pass on to every soul that you meet, speak to, think of and connect with in any way. It will gently ignite the light within their own cells and remind them of who they really are.

Step 6

The Elemental Dragons

Dragons are fourth-dimensional elementals. They act as companions and friends and are always ready to help and protect us. They can also operate on different dimensions; in other words, they move between the wavelengths, altering their frequency as they do so. This means that they can transmute very low-frequency third-dimensional stuck energy and they are therefore incredibly important in the clearance process preparing us for ascension.

All dragons originated in Lemuria. Because the Lemurians so loved the Earth and nature, the dragons served them by keeping the frequency on the planet very high and pure. Dragons have been available to help us ever since that age.

Dragons can be small or they can expand to an enormous size if necessary. They also change colour, depending on the energy they need to use.

Just like angels, dragons have names. We can ask a dragon for its name and it will drop it into our mind. This creates a more personal bond between us.

Fire Dragons

Fire dragons are commanded by the elemental master Thor. The entire element of fire is overseen by Archangel Gabriel because of the wonderful quality of purification he represents. Because fire transmutes negativity, these dragons are perfect companions for those undertaking challenging spiritual work.

You can ask fire dragons to burn up negativity in your chakras, especially if you have been undergoing lessons. This will enable you to see clearly the message within the challenge. If you have been in a low place, either physically or emotionally, they will do an excellent job of cleansing anything you have picked up in your centres. Many lightworkers are very sensitive and open, so they unwittingly allow lower energies to enter their aura. Fire dragons will do a heroic job of clearing these if you ask them.

You can always send fire dragons to war zones, where, like combat forces, they dive into the heavy frequencies to burn them up.

In addition, if your birth sign is a fire sign, you will have your own personal fire dragon. Depending on your life mission, you may have been allocated a fire dragon even if you are a different astrological sign. A fire dragon will, however, come to anyone who is in need of that element of spiritual assistance. More and more people are working with them as the transitions on Earth intensify.

Air, water and earth dragons tend to work more intensely with the structures surrounding us. They will also assist when called upon.

Water Dragons
Really these are water serpents. They are shimmering blue, green or silver and carry feminine energy. Commanded by the great \ Masters Neptune and Odin, with Poseidon in overall charge, they are the keepers of the fifth-dimensional records of the sea and help to keep in place the sacred geometry of the waters.

You can call water serpents in to raise the frequency of local water sources. They will also help you develop and express your personal creativity.

Air Dragons

The elemental master of air is Dom, and he commands the air dragons, with the unicorns in overall charge.

The air dragons work via the wind to push out the old and allow the new to come in. They literally act as a breath of fresh air over cities or other places where energy becomes stuck or stagnant.

Unicorns are at the forefront of gales, storms and hurricanes, followed by the air dragons, who help to bring in the geometric structure of the replacement energy. They create spirals of energy to ensure higher frequencies keep moving in.

Earth Dragons

The elemental master of Earth is Taia. She commands the earth dragons and Lady Gaia is in overall charge of them. These mighty elementals protect the ley lines. They can fire them up to purify them, especially after disruptions like earthquakes.

How to Work with Dragons

As with all beings from other realms who are sent to assist us, to work with dragons you must apply the golden rule: ask for their help. You will then receive it if it is for your highest good.

If you have nightmares (in other words, if you are entering the lower astral, where emotions and worry thought-forms are stored), you can ask a fire dragon to accompany you when you sleep and protect you. The fire dragon will burn up the lower frequencies before your spirit passes through them. This can be really helpful for sensitive children.

If you want help with artistic or creative work, or even with the general flow of your life, call on a water dragon to become your companion and helper.

If you are ready to move forward or want a stuck situation to be released, ask the air dragons to blow the old away and bring in something higher.

You can do important service work by asking the earth dragons to protect the ley lines. This may even prevent earthquakes from happening. When you visit sacred sites you can also activate the earth dragons there to hold the frequency high and steady.

How to Serve a Dragon

As with all things on Earth, energy flows two ways, so it is appropriate to give to dragons as well as to receive.

- Dragons love healing, so hold them in healing thoughts. Every so often light a candle for them or hold a healing ceremony for them. This will help to inspire and empower them for, like us, they love to be acknowledged. Elementals have feelings, as we do.

- Tell people about them.

- Write about them! Children especially love dragon stories.

- Draw a dragon.

- Purchase a model dragon.

Always remember to thank the dragons when you have asked them to serve you. You might like to do it with the following ceremony:

Dragon Thanking Ceremony

1. Place a little table in the centre of a room and cover it with a pretty cloth if you can.

2. Light a candle and place it at the centre of the table.

3. As you do so, say:

    'I dedicate this fire to the fire dragons with thanks for all they do.'

4. Place a small bowl of pure water on the table.

5. As you do so, hold your hands over it and bless it with the words:

'I bless this water with thanks to the water dragons for all they do.'

6. Place a feather or leaf on the table.

7. Bless it with the words:

   'I bless the air with thanks to the air dragons for all they do.'

8. Hold a pebble or crystal in your hands.

9. Say:

   'I bless this pebble/crystal with thanks to the earth dragons for all they do.'

10. Place it on the table.

11. Pick up the candle and walk clockwise round the table three times.

12. Blow out the candle and the dragons will be celebrating with delight.

Fifth-Dimensional Golden Dragons

At the Cosmic Moment a team of fifth-dimensional golden dragons came forward. These beings do not represent the elements, like the fourth-dimensional dragons. They are here to support and protect our ascension. For example, if there is a sacred ceremony or spiritual gathering, these golden beings will circle it, so that the energy is maintained within it at a fifth-dimensional frequency.

Recently the cosmic portal of Honolulu opened and a flood of dragons emerged, ready to assist us with the ascension process. In addition the cosmic portal of Andorra, which is a great dragon portal, has now opened. As a result, dragon energy is spreading over Europe.

Letters to the Dragons

Below are examples of letters you can write to your dragons. You can change or expand these as you wish. Please remember that they are a powerful form of communication and activation.

Dragons have great personalities and like to be addressed individually. Also, they are very big on manners!

Fire Dragon Activation Letter

You can do this verbally, but it is more powerful to write a letter. Here is an example. The best way of sending the energy of your letter to the dragon world is to burn it carefully.

Beloved Fire Dragon,

I call to you now to assist me with my ascension journey on this planet. At this moment in time and from now on, I greatly need your loving service.

I ask that you keep the energy around me clear and fifth-dimensional at all times, not just in my waking hours, but also on the inner planes.

I ask that you accompany me wherever I go and, if I am busy and distracted, alert me to intrusions and drops in my frequency.

This is, I know, a lot of work and I humbly thank you for your assistance.

Finally I ask you to protect my home and the physical, mental, emotional and spiritual energies of my family [give their names].

As I progress on my spiritual path, so will you, and together we will bring in the light as Earth and humanity rise to another level.

Our relationship will always be two-way. Anything that you require of me in return, please ask, and know that my home is your home also.

With my unconditional love and gratitude,

[Sign your name.]

Letter to an Earth Dragon

Again you can talk to your dragon, but a letter has more power and energy.

Beloved Earth Dragon,

I offer you thanks for keeping the earth under my home clear and safe. I want my living accommodation to be a fifth-dimensional portal of radiant light and I ask that you hold the basis for this to be so. Please work with the fire dragons to burn up any lower energies that are under my home.

I ask you to keep the ley lines between the sacred sites in my country [or the world] clear and pure.

Thank you for your service.

With my love and gratitude,

[Sign your name.]

Letter to an Air Dragon

Beloved Air Dragon,

Please work with me to keep my aura sparkling and clear at all times.

I ask you to keep a spiral of energy moving through my home, constantly replacing what is there with a fresh higher energy. Move through every room of my house daily, sweeping away etheric cobwebs or dust.

I also ask you to extend this service to the world.

Thank you for your service.

With my love and gratitude,

[Sign your name.]

Letter to a Water Dragon

Beloved Water Dragon,

I ask you to move through the waters of the world, clearing and cleansing and purifying them, so that love can travel freely everywhere.

I ask you to bless and purify every drop of water that enters my house, including in the atmosphere.

Please bless and purify the water in the cells of my body and ensure that all the water surrounding me and within me resonates at a fifth-dimensional frequency.

Thank you for your service.

With my love and gratitude,

[Sign your name]

Step 7

The Elemental Kingdom

The elemental kingdom is an essential part of the divine plan for Earth. It is intimately related to the angelic kingdom. The elementals are the younger brothers of the angels. These little ethereal creatures are known as elementals because they do not have all four elements. Some, like fairies, contain only one element:

- Fairies and sylphs are air elementals.

- Goblins, pixies and elves are earth elementals.

- Fire dragons and salamanders are fire elementals.

- Undines and mermaids are water elementals.

- Imps and fauns are mixed elementals.

Until the Cosmic Moment in 2012 the elementals ranged between the third and the fifth dimension. As the frequency of the planet has been rapidly rising since that time, the third-dimensional elementals who have been serving the planet for aeons have moved into the fourth dimension. Those who have recently come to Earth, like the kyhils, who are clearing pollution in our waters, and the esaks, who are cleansing stuck energy on the land, have not yet had an opportunity to open their hearts to the fourth-dimensional paradigm, but they very soon will.

Once the fifth-dimensional elementals – some fairies, goblins and some dragons – have been through their initiations on the planet, they will be given the opportunity to ascend to the seventh dimension to join the ranks of the angels.

The elementals are ascending very quickly as they prepare the infrastructure of the Earth by tending the trees and plants and raising the vibration of the land and the soil itself.

The earth elementals hold sacred geometric structures within the land. As the new Golden Age approaches, the earth dragons are waking up. They are lighting up the wisdom contained within the crystals planted deep in the Earth during the time of Lemuria. These crystals are activating sacred geometric light codes and these are then projected into the Earth merkabah. The earth dragons are now activating a planetary merkabah ignition.

The wonderful, wise and big-hearted fifth-dimensional goblins have now anchored the dragon line energy that forms a grid around the world. A dragon line is a line of flowing energy that replaces the old ley-line system but does not have the seventh-dimensional frequency of the new crystalline grid.

The trees are keepers of local knowledge and wisdom. The goblins are passing the knowledge and wisdom held within the trees of the world, as well as other energies, through this grid to program it for the New Age. They have also started the process of taking the light from other star systems that is currently stored in our huge forests and directing this down the grid. This is only a fraction of the light that will flow through the dragon lines as the infrastructure of the New Age is completed.

As the earth elementals, the elves, pixies and goblins, are raising their frequency, they are igniting the codes in the soil and bringing up the vibration within which the plants grow. Consequently our food is rising in frequency.

During this intense period of creation, the elementals, under the direction of the elemental masters and their commanders, are raising the frequency of the entire nature kingdom:

- The elemental master of air is Dom, overseen by the unicorns.

- The elemental master of fire is Thor, overseen by Archangel Gabriel.

- The elemental master of earth is Taia, overseen by Lady Gaia.

- The elemental master of water is Neptune, overseen by Poseidon.

- In charge of the entire process is Archangel Gabriel, who co-ordinates with Pan, a ninth-dimensional master, and Archangel Purlimiek, the angel of nature.

- Archangel Metatron is the commander-in-chief.

As the frequency of nature is speeding up it is raising our human frequency at a cellular level by harmonic transference. In addition, the light from the Sun is illuminating the cells of our body and this, together with the shifting frequencies of nature, is automatically changing the structure of our DNA from a two-strand DNA system to the 12-strand system that they had in the Golden Era of Atlantis. In this way the awesome gifts, talents and powers that we had in that era are being returned to us.

More and more unicorns are now pouring from the heart of Source to Earth. The seventh-dimensional unicorns were the first to return here to shower their light and love onto us. Now the ninth-dimensional ones are blessing us with their presence. They are entering through Archangel Christiel's stargate, high in the etheric above Tibet.

Earth
As the earth dragons rest above the Earth, their light, containing the love and wisdom codes of Source, is directed in a shaft to the ground. The fairies anchor it, then the goblins take it down into Hollow Earth to be spread through the crystalline grid.

Water
The water dragons, who are really water serpents, are holding a new vibrational structure within the waters of the Earth. The

planetary waters were illuminated at the Cosmic Moment with a light dispensation of galactic intensity which increased the Christ consciousness within the water and added pure golden light. This started the process of planetary change, as water flows everywhere, permeating everything.

The great master Neptune is singing the fifth-dimensional notes and holding the resonance of the Christ consciousness for the water. This enables the undines, the water elementals, to maintain the harmonic of the Christ consciousness frequency within the oceans and spread it through the energetic tidal flows governed by the lunar cycles.

At every full Moon incredible frequencies are being projected into the seas, rivers and lakes of the planet, reflecting pure angelic love and the codes of Helios. With each succeeding full Moon, the vibration of the water is rising higher. This includes the water within the cells of humans.

Fire

Fire is the most powerful alchemically transformational force on this planet. It has always been used on Earth to transmute third-dimensional frequencies into a higher form. This is currently happening all over the world as a fast-track method of removing pockets of density.

The salamanders and fire dragons, the elementals of fire, under direction from Thor, the elemental master of fire, are path-clearing rapidly to ensure that the Christ consciousness can flow wherever possible.

In addition fire dragons are being sent into very dense areas. It is the task of humans to create, with their thoughts, the bridges that allow the fire dragons to enter these areas. When they have transmuted lower frequencies, we can call in the unicorns and Archangel Christiel's angels to illuminate the cleansed area with hope and inspiration.

Visualization to Align with the Elementals to Purify Parts of the Planet

1. Prepare a space where you can be relaxed and undisturbed. You may like to be out in nature.

2. Sit quietly and breathe comfortably with the intention of connecting with the elementals to raise the frequency of the world.

3. Ground yourself by visualizing roots going from your feet deep into the Earth.

4. Ask Archangel Michael to place his deep blue cloak of protection around you.

5. Invoke Thor, master of fire, to bring to you the fire dragons and the salamanders. Send them into an area that needs higher light. Visualize them burning away the lower energies.

6. Call upon Dom, master of air, to send the wind elementals, sylphs, fairies and air dragons to fan the flames of transmutation.

7. Call in Neptune, master of water, to bring the undines and rain to purify the area until it is sparkling clean. See the shimmering rain washing into the earth.

8. Call in Taia, master of earth, to send the earth dragons to spread the new vibration through the land at this place.

9. Call in the unicorns and Archangel Christiel's angels to illuminate the area permanently with Christ Light, hope, inspiration and pure love.

10. Thank the elemental masters and the elementals for all their service work.

11. Open your eyes and know you have accelerated the ascension of the planet with the help of the elementals.

Step 8

The Intergalactic Council

The Intergalactic Council is a body of 12 mighty beings who take decisions for the evolution of Earth. They decide on and oversee great experiments, like that of Atlantis, which was to see if humans could maintain a physical body, experience emotions and keep a connection with Source.

Because the frequency has risen so much in recent years, individuals and groups can now connect with the Intergalactic Council via Archangel Butyalil to petition for help for the planet or for a project of importance to the health, welfare or advancement of humanity. We can also offer our services to help the world or the universe.

Those currently serving on the Council are:

Master Marko

The great Master Marko represents the highest galactic confederation in the solar system. He holds all the technological information of the united universes within a huge, very high-frequency quartz crystal skull and he downloads appropriate ideas into the minds of those who are ready to bring fifth-dimensional technology back to the planet. The information is already stored in the etheric and also within the soul star chakras of those serving in this way. An example is digital cameras, which capture the sixth-dimensional frequency of angelic beings as Orbs.

The scientific establishment is just discovering the existence of parallel worlds. Once it has accepted that science and spirituality work hand in hand, scientists will be ready to receive a higher grade of information. Master Marko is monitoring this very carefully with the help of Seraphina the Seraphim.

Commander Ashtar

Commander Ashtar is the seventh-dimensional commander of the Intergalactic Fleet, whose spaceships patrol the area around Earth to protect and assist us. They are not visible to us because of their high frequency.

Commander Ashtar is working hand in hand with Archangel Metatron to assist with the ascension process. He will be waiting to greet millions of souls when they have achieved their ascension. He looks after the great two-way inter-dimensional portal of Machu Picchu, Peru, and his mother ship enters our planet through this portal. His role on the Intergalactic Council is to maintain the equilibrium of the universes to keep them in balance and harmony with one another.

Lord Hilarion

Lord Hilarion, the master of the Fifth Ray, the Orange Ray of Technology and Science, works closely with Master Marko and Commander Ashtar. These three co-operate to see that appropriate information is downloaded into the minds of those who are ready to work with it. Examples are the new communication technologies, Orb photography, crystal technology and clean power.

If you have a concept for spiritual technology to help humanity, be aware that Lord Hilarion or one of Archangel Raphael's angels who works with him has dropped it into your consciousness. You can ask him to help you bring it forward and oversee its progression.

St Germain

St Germain, who has recently been promoted to Lord of Civilization, a high-ranking post in the spiritual hierarchy, is also the Ascended Keeper of the Cosmic Diamond Violet Flame, along with Archangels Gabriel and Zadkiel. This flame has the power to transmute lower energies into very high frequencies.

St Germain's role on the Intergalactic Council is to civilize humanity! He holds the divine fifth-dimensional blueprint for the communities and golden cities of the new Golden Age to come. He is re-establishing the way of life that people enjoyed in the Golden Era of Atlantis, only at a higher level.

Jesus

Jesus, in his new ninth-dimensional role of Bringer of Cosmic Love, is literally spreading the Christ Light of the 33 vibration to the whole planet. (Thirty-three is the number that resonates with the Christ consciousness frequency.) His chakras are connected with the Cosmic Heart and he is overseeing the heart activation of the entire world.

His role on the Intergalactic Council is to plant the seeds of pure love wherever they can grow. He works with Archangel Christiel, who is awakening humanity to higher love.

Quan Yin

Quan Yin, known as the Goddess of Mercy, had a 2,000-year incarnation in China and has a vast influence on the world. She is also Lord of Karma for the Sixth Ray of Loving, Devoted Service, co-operating with Archangel Uriel.

Her role on the Intergalactic Council is to spread the Divine Feminine wisdom everywhere, to empower women and to allow men to become more in touch with their feminine side. She is also helping to bring forward the balance of ascending Earth. Once this is established on our planet, her role on the Intergalactic Council will change and she will focus on the ascension of another planet.

Lord Kuthumi

Lord Kuthumi is now the world teacher in charge of all the teaching establishments in the inner planes. He also supervises the Hollow Earth University for planetary leaders and on Earth is preparing us for higher-quality leadership. He is also working with Archangel Jophiel, archangel of wisdom, helping us to see our children differently so that we can allow in education systems that nurture the special beings that are being entrusted to our care now.

El Morya

El Morya is the master of the First Ray of Divine Will and Creation. His role on the Intergalactic Council is to strengthen our divine will so that we can actively create the new Golden Age. With Archangel Michael, he is holding the fifth-dimensional blueprint for those who incarnate as males in the society of the future, so that they can demonstrate masculine energy in perfect balance with their Divine Feminine energy.

With Archangel Faith, El Morya is also touching all females and helping them to balance their masculine and feminine energy. He holds the collective vision for the fifth-dimensional distribution of power so that the male–female balance is correct.

At this present moment in time he is helping to disassemble the existing ego structure that has surrounded Earth since the fall of Atlantis.

Serapis Bey

Serapis Bey is the master of the Fourth Ray of Harmony and Balance, co-operating with Archangel Gabriel. He was a great priest avatar in Atlantis and is Keeper of the White Ascension Flame of Atlantis, which represents the pinnacle of purity achieved by alignment to Christ consciousness, on behalf of the Intergalactic Council. He also works with Lord Maitreya to oversee the various White Brotherhoods throughout the universe.

All over the planet there are pyramids that contain different resonances of the Ascension Flame. When we reach a certain frequency, Serapis Bey will bring them together into one glorious Ascension Flame and this will form the crystalline matrix of ascended Gaia – in other words, it will activate the new energy body of our planet. When humanity reaches the upper levels of the fifth dimension, Serapis Bey will step in to help people maintain their frequency at this high level.

Paul the Venetian
Paul the Venetian is the master of the Third Ray of Creativity and Artistic Expression. He works with Archangel Chamuel to bring love into people's manifestations. His energy flows through writers, artists and creative initiators of all kinds to bring ascension light through their endeavours. These works born in pure love will spread ascension energy for as long as they are in physical existence and never lose their resonance.

Paul the Venetian's task on the Intergalactic Council is to help us understand the importance of creativity. Creativity is the foundation of manifestation in our new world.

Mary Magdalene
Lady Nada served the Intergalactic Council for centuries and was very focused on Earth. She is now spreading cosmic love to the universe and Mary Magdalene has been promoted to take her place, with the assistance of Lady Portia, goddess of justice.

Mary Magdalene is working with Archangel Uriel to bring spirituality into religions in which the consciousness needs to shift to the fifth-dimensional frequency. Her task on the Intergalactic Council is to hold the vision of unified love.

Lord Maitreya
Lord Maitreya is the master of the Great White Brotherhood. The Maitreya energy is the blueprint of peace on Earth. His task on the Intergalactic Council is to hold the vision of peace and he

works with the unicorns and Archangel Christiel to bring this to physical reality on our planet.

Visualization to Connect to the Intergalactic Council

If you wish to visit the Intergalactic Council, you can ask Archangel Butyalil to take you to their temple in the inner planes. If you feel particularly attracted to the energy of an individual member of the Council, you can also connect to them personally.

To prepare for the connection, during the day say the names of the masters on the Intergalactic Council. Learn who they are and feel their individual resonance.

1. Prepare a space where you can be relaxed and undisturbed. Light a candle if you can.

2. Sit quietly and breathe comfortably with the intention of visiting the Intergalactic Council.

3. Ground yourself by visualizing roots going from your feet deep into the Earth.

4. Ask Archangel Michael to place his deep blue cloak of protection around you.

5. Ask Archangel Butyalil to come to you and place his pure white light around you. Breathe in his high-frequency energy.

6. Archangel Butyalil is taking you to the Intergalactic Council. Instantly you find yourself in a blindingly clear light surrounded by 12 indescribable Illumined Beings. Be aware that their light is opening you up to higher frequencies.

7. One of the masters steps forward. You recognize them.

8. They place one hand on your crown chakra and the other on your heart. Your chakras unify into a column of light.

9. Within your 12 chakras is a facet of each master present on the Council. You will carry this energy on your ascension mission.

10. You now have permission to visit the Intergalactic Council whenever you wish in order to assist the planet. You are one of their representatives on Earth and can use this power to assist the universe.

11. Open your eyes, breathe deeply and spread your beautiful light.

In fact you may already be a representative of the Intergalactic Council here on Earth before doing this visualization. You may be consciously aware of this or you may be doing heroic service during your sleep and be completely unconscious of it.

Step 9

Petition the Intergalactic Council to Help the World

Because we have free will the Intergalactic Council cannot do anything directly to our consciousness, but they can change the energy around us. This is rather like changing the soil round a plant so that it can grow abundantly. You can petition the Council to change the energy to help all of us here on Earth at this time.

Here are some examples of what you can ask for. The more people who tune in to these requests and add their energy to them, the more quickly the whole planet will move forward.

Unconditional Love
Unconditional love, the 33 vibration of Christ consciousness, will eventually be established fully in accordance with the higher crystalline matrix, the new high-frequency structure of the planet. If we can accelerate this process, the whole world will be happy and radiate open-hearted love and acceptance more quickly. We can visit the Intergalactic Council and ask them to help us become a conduit for the Christ consciousness so that we can spread it into the crystalline matrix. Every individual who does this is taking responsibility for their part in transforming Earth into a planet of love. This is the new agape paradigm. Agape means pure, unconditional love.

Worldwide Peace

Worldwide peace will be achieved when the Divine Feminine is fully balanced on the planet. We can ask the Intergalactic Council to amplify the Divine Feminine energies throughout the world. This will mean that full Moons are even more powerful times for drawing in this energy. Therefore it is important at the same time to invoke Archangel Sandalphon to strengthen the power of the tourmaline and haematite crystals within the planet to keep everyone grounded.

There are also other steps that can accelerate peace:

- We can ask the Intergalactic Council for a huge dispensation to saturate the planet with the Cosmic Diamond Violet Flame, amplified by the seven cosmic pyramids that originally formed part of the dome of Atlantis and are now placed around Earth.

- We can invoke Quan Yin, Lady Nada, Mary Magdalene and Lady Portia to place a diamond in the energy fields of every single female on the planet so that they connect heart to heart in an unbreakable sisterhood of support and mutual empowerment. This will enable women to take their rightful roles and bring the divine masculine and feminine into balance on the planet.

- We can also ask that more fire dragons are made available to burn up the lower energies on Earth and that humans are prompted to send them into the places where they are needed.

The Children and Education

The crystal pyramids that formed the dome over Golden Atlantis have now been placed around the universe. Some are strategically positioned over sacred areas on Earth, such as Sedona, Mount Shasta, Uluru and Tibet, to keep the frequency high.

Many people recognize it is time to treat children as individuals, raising and educating them so that their physical, emotional, mental and spiritual needs are met and nurtured. It is time to hold the intention of bringing up generations of happy, enlightened, peaceful children who are able to develop their potential in the highest possible way.

So we can ask that a crystal pyramid containing the knowledge and wisdom to do this is made available. We can ask for it to be located over Earth, where its light can bathe everyone in increasing waves, and that as this occurs Archangel Sandalphon sends a grounding energy to humanity, so that we can activate the new ways.

Animals
We can give thanks for the mighty portal for animals that opened in Yellowstone in 2012 and ask the Intergalactic Council for more portals for animals to be placed on each continent, all radiating the yellow energy of Archangel Fhelyai, angel of animals, to raise the consciousness of humanity towards animals and help animals to increase their confidence and self-worth.

New Spiritual Technology
We can ask that seed thoughts of new spiritual technology to power the planet in a fifth-dimensional way be placed in the minds of individuals who are prepared for this work. Seeds need perfect soil and nutrients in order to grow, so we can ask that round each seed thought are placed the energies that enable it to propagate and blossom.

There are many other appropriate requests that you can make to the Intergalactic Council, but we have discussed those above with the members of the Council. If enough people petition them, they will grant these wishes and others in a way that will be for the highest good.

Visualization to Petition the Intergalactic Council

1. Prepare a space where you can be relaxed and undisturbed. Light a candle if you can.

2. Sit quietly and breathe comfortably with the intention of visiting the Intergalactic Council with a petition to accelerate the ascension of the planet.

3. Ground yourself by visualizing roots going from your feet deep into the Earth.

4. Ask Archangel Michael to place his deep blue cloak of protection around you.

5. Be aware of Archangel Butyalil standing in front of you as a pure white light, or look at his Orb. Step into his energy and breathe it in. Your latent intergalactic connection ability is being illuminated.

6. Surrounded by Archangel Butyalil's pure white light, you are ascending through the dimensions until you see the etheric castle of the Intergalactic Council's retreat in front of you.

7. Either mentally or out loud, invoke the 12 Illumined Masters. Feel them come to you and greet each one individually. They form a high-frequency circle of which you are now a part.

8. Either mentally or out loud, make your petition to the Council, then remain quiet as they consider your request.

9. One of them will now speak to you. Jesus is usually the vocal representative. He is wise, unconditionally loving and kind beyond measure. He understands humanity very well and holds Earth to be his highest priority. He will let you know if your request for the planet has been granted in Divine Order, that is, exactly as it should when in flow with Source energy.

10. In the centre of the circle of 12 there appears a globe of light. Here you can see the energy of the petitions for this request gathering.

11. Jesus takes you to look through a diamond window. You look down on Earth and see the impact of your request when it is fully actioned.

12. The 12 bow to you and thank you for using your light to help your planet. A light from each of them enters your heart and you feel it.

13. Thank them.

14. Step again into Archangel Butyalil's pure white light and return to where you started.

Step 10

The Cosmic Diamond Violet Flame

At the fall of Atlantis the mighty Violet Flame, with its great power to transmute lower energies into very high frequencies, was misused and consequently the Intergalactic Council withdrew it, so that it could no longer be utilized by the masses. In 1987, at the Harmonic Convergence, Archangel Zadkiel and St Germain petitioned Source for its return and they reintroduced it to the whole of humanity. A few years later it became the Silver Violet Flame as the silver light of grace and Divine Feminine energy were added to it. Then we earned the right for the Gold Flame of Wisdom to merge with it, so that it became the Gold and Silver Violet Flame.

Now Archangel Zadkiel and St Germain have once more upgraded the Gold and Silver Violet Flame of transmutation. When we use the Cosmic Diamond Violet Flame it fully clears and transmutes the old into pure, luminous Source light.

Angels often tell us to look at how far we have come and rejoice in how much we have achieved, rather than to look forward and wonder what we have yet to attain. The Cosmic Diamond Violet Flame of transmutation reminds us how much we have accomplished on our glorious journey to ascension.

I AM

I AM prayers are a very high form of affirmation or invocation. We literally call on our Monad or I AM Presence to merge with the being or energy we are invoking. The following was given to Diana by Archangel Zadkiel as she walked along the beach many years ago. It was set beautifully to music by Rosemary Stephenson.

'I AM the Gold and Silver Violet Flame.
I AM the Flame of Mercy.
I AM the Flame of Joy.
I AM the Flame of Transmutation.
I AM St Germain.
I AM Archangel Zadkiel.'

Since then the frequency on the planet has become much faster. The Gold and Silver Flame has now evolved and Archangels Gabriel and Zadkiel have united their energies to form the Cosmic Diamond Violet Flame. The grace and harmony of the Silver Flame are still within it, as are the wisdom, love and healing of the golden ray, but the faster frequency has transcended the previous light.

Now Archangel Gabriel's great Cosmic Diamond, lit up by Archangel Zadkiel's violet light, can be placed over us, or any person or place. It will take the old into the heart of Source for clearance. Its energy does not only transmute, it also cuts away the old with the incisive power and clarity of a diamond and raises everything to the fifth dimension and above.

Here is a new affirmation, which can be sung to the tune of the former one:

'I AM the Cosmic Diamond Violet Flame.
I AM the Flame of Mercy.
I AM the Flame of Joy.
I AM the Flame of Oneness.
I AM St Germain.
I AM Gabriel Zadkiel.'

Uses of the Cosmic Diamond Violet Flame
We can use the Cosmic Diamond Violet Flame in a number of ways:

- We can invoke it and ask it to purify and clarify the path in front of us. Because of the precision of its light, it can shred the frequency of potential problems then raise them so that they no longer exist. If we call in the fire dragons to blaze a trail of fire in front of us, followed by the Cosmic Diamond Violet Flame, we will have a tremendously effective army of light preceding us.

- We can visualize this flame over ourselves to transmute any lower energies within us or around us and these will be transformed into the brilliance of a diamond. This also affects physical disease or blocks.

- We can send it to those who are sick or depressed – but we should use our intuition as to whether this is the right energy to use, for it is incredibly powerful and might overpower some people.

- Where relationships lack harmony, the Cosmic Diamond Violet Flame cuts through the negativity with blades of ice. The resultant clear space gives the opponents an opportunity to look at the situation from a higher perspective.

- It is always helpful to send this flame to purify the energy of war. If you are doing this, ensure that you ask it to go deep into the Earth in such places to light up the ley lines and the ground itself.

- As the frequency of humanity and the planet rises, we must heal and clarify the communication networks. One effective way is to send the Cosmic Diamond Violet Flame along telephone lines and through the internet.

- There are many souls who have not passed over properly and they are clogging up the astral planes. In addition to forming columns of light through which they can pass or asking the angels to collect them, we can really assist by visualizing the Cosmic Diamond Violet Flame filling the astral planes, so that stuck souls seek the light. Archangels Gabriel and Zadkiel will lead back home those who are lost.

Fire and Ice

The symbol of the new Golden Age is the sacred geometric shape of Metatron's Cube or his six-pointed star, and when you use this in conjunction with the Cosmic Diamond Violet Flame you have a potent ascension tool.

You are combining Archangel Metatron's fire with the ice of the diamond.

Visualization to Work with the Metatron Star

1. The Metatron star is six-pointed. Visualize a central point with six lines like spokes radiating from it, one up, one down and two from each side.
2. In the centre see the great diamond shimmering with violet light.
3. Invoke this to raise the frequency of our beautiful planet and all its inhabitants, woodlands, oceans and inner planes.

Visualization to Work with the Cosmic Diamond Violet Flame

1. Prepare a space where you can be relaxed and undisturbed. Light a candle if you can.
2. Sit quietly and breathe comfortably with the intention of working with the Cosmic Diamond Violet Flame.
3. Ground yourself by visualizing roots going from your feet deep into the Earth.
4. Ask Archangel Michael to place his deep blue cloak of protection around you.

5. With your heart as the central point, picture a star of Metatron fire lines radiating from you.

6. Invoke the Cosmic Diamond Violet Flame and see the vast diamond, shimmering violet, being placed over your energy fields. Rest in this energy as you are being purified.

7. Ask the Cosmic Diamond Violet Flame to clear the path in front of you throughout your day and night.

8. If it feels right, visualize the Cosmic Diamond Violet Flame over someone who is ill or depressed. Sense them lighting up.

9. Place the six-pointed Metatron star and the Cosmic Diamond Violet Flame over any areas where there is lower energy and in the astral planes.

10. Send it to the communication networks, ley lines, worldwide web and telephone lines of the world.

11. Imagine a vast Cosmic Diamond Violet Flame over the entire planet being held by thousands of Archangel Gabriel and Archangel Zadkiel's angels. They will be singing the higher purification into the heart of Source.

12. Thank the Archangels and open your eyes.

Step 11

Access Stellar Wisdom

Aspects of each of our chakras vibrate at different frequencies and connect to a variety of dimensions. Planets, stars and galaxies are themselves all chakras of the cosmos. When our 12 fifth-dimensional chakras are awake and operational, we can connect each one to the appropriate star and start to access and download the codes of light it emits. When we do this, we can become an intergalactic master. We will be overseen, both during the process and afterwards, by Seraphina, one of the mighty Seraphim.

Just like humans, aspects of the planets, stars and galaxies have fully ascended and radiate a very high-frequency energy. They hold the divine blueprint and divine vision for the universe. Others have partially ascended, in which case only the ascended aspect radiates a seventh-dimensional light.

It is necessary to learn how to link our chakras to the stars because many more lightworkers will be working on an intergalactic level in future years and this will be an essential aspect for many of becoming an ascended master.

When a sufficient number of people have connected to the heart of the stars, the energy will enable a high-frequency portal in northern China to awaken. Once open, this will radiate a pure white Source love to help everyone on the planet and assist Gaia with her transition to the Golden Age.

When you link your chakras to the stars, you not only become a vast galactic master but your aura extends round the universe. In order to activate the link, you must have your 12 chakras open and blazing with light. The process is as follows:

Connecting Your Chakras to the Stars

1. Prepare a space where you can relax and be undisturbed. Light a candle if you can.
2. Sit quietly and breathe comfortably with the intention of connecting your chakras to the hearts of the stars.
3. Ground yourself by visualizing roots going from your feet deep into the Earth.
4. Ask Archangel Michael to place his deep blue cloak of protection around you.

The Earth Star

1. Focus on your Earth Star chakra below your feet.
2. Call in Archangel Sandalphon to open this chakra and light up the black-and-white ball that is your foundation and holds your divine potential.
3. Send light from here to the planetary Earth Star chakra in London, UK, and visualize the White Ascension Flame burning there.
4. Imagine a link connecting your Earth Star chakra to the planet Neptune.
5. Be aware of the light codes containing the wisdom of Atlantis and Lemuria flowing from Neptune into your Earth Star chakra.
6. Take the frequency higher and link into the ascended aspect of Neptune, called Toutillay.
7. Feel the higher vibration of the name flow through you as you say the name 'Toutillay' to yourself three times: 'Toutillay. Toutillay. Toutillay.'
8. Start to draw down the cosmic light for this universe.
9. Sense it lighting up your Earth Star chakra.

The Base Chakra

1. Focus on your base chakra and call in Archangel Gabriel to open it and light it up into a beautiful shimmering platinum ball.

2. Send light from here to the planetary base chakra in northern China and visualize an ascension flame burning there.

3. Now imagine a link connecting your base chakra to Saturn.

4. Take the frequency higher and link to the ascended aspect of Saturn, called Quishy.

5. Feel the higher vibration of Quishy flow through you as you say the name to yourself three times: 'Quishy. Quishy. Quishy.'

6. It is radiating the energy of spiritual discipline to enable you to fulfil your divine potential. It enables you to enjoy the delight of being on Earth by linking you to your original divine essence. Relax and absorb this light.

The Sacral Chakra

1. Focus on your sacral chakra and call in Archangel Gabriel to open it and light it up into a wondrous shining pink ball.

2. Send light from here to the planetary sacral chakra in Honolulu, and visualize an ascension flame burning there.

3. Now imagine a link connecting your sacral chakra to Sirius.

4. Take the frequency higher and link into the ascended aspect of Sirius, called Lakumay.

5. Feel the higher vibration of Lakumay flow through you as you say the name to yourself three times: 'Lakumay. Lakumay. Lakumay.'

6. It is pouring pure transcendent love into your chakra. Relax and absorb it.

The Navel Chakra

1. Focus on your navel chakra and call in Archangel Gabriel to open it and light it up into a glorious glowing orange ball.

2. Send light from here to the planetary navel chakra in Fiji, in the Pacific Islands, and visualize an ascension flame burning there.

3. Now imagine a link connecting your navel chakra to the Sun, which is fully ascended.

4. Feel the higher vibration of the Sun flow through you as you say it to yourself three times: 'Sun. Sun. Sun.'

5. Sense the golden orange light waking up your navel chakra so that you can go out and actively make people feel welcome.

6. This energy will open you up to beings from other planets and enable you to accept their wisdom. Relax and feel it lighting up your navel chakra.

The Solar Plexus Chakra

1. Focus on your solar plexus chakra and call in Archangel Uriel to open it and light it up into a magnificent deep golden ball.

2. Send light from here to the planetary solar plexus chakra in the whole of South Africa and visualize an ascension flame burning there.

3. Now imagine a link connecting your solar plexus chakra to the centre of the Earth.

4. Take the frequency higher and link to the ascended aspect of Earth, called Pilchay.

5. Feel the higher vibration of Pilchay flow through you as you say the name to yourself three times: 'Pilchay. Pilchay. Pilchay.'

6. Sense the golden light waking up your solar plexus chakra so that you access the cosmic wisdom waiting to come in. Relax and feel it lighting up your solar plexus chakra.

The Heart Chakra

1. Focus on your heart chakra and call in Archangel Chamuel to open it and light it up until it is a blazing white light with pale pink infused in it.

2. Send light from here to the planetary heart chakra in Glastonbury, UK, and visualize an ascension flame burning there.

3. Now imagine a link connecting your heart chakra to the Cosmic Heart chakra, Venus. This has ascended and brings love directly from God.

4. Feel the vibration of Venus flow through you as you say its name to yourself three times: 'Venus. Venus. Venus.'

5. Sense the pure white light flowing into your heart chakra.

6. Relax and know that you are open to the love of God.

The Throat Chakra

1. Focus on your throat chakra and call in Archangel Michael to open it and light it up into a majestic royal-blue ball.

2. Send light from here to the planetary throat chakra in Luxor, Egypt, and visualize an ascension flame burning there.

3. Now imagine a link connecting your throat chakra to Mercury.

4. Take the energy higher and link to Telephony, the ascended aspect of Mercury.

5. Feel the higher vibration of Telephony flow through you as you say the name to yourself three times: 'Telephony. Telephony. Telephony.'

6. Sense the glorious blue light waking up your throat chakra.

7. Draw in your gifts of telepathic communication with the masters and angels on the golden ray.

8. Draw in the energy to communicate with humans, animals, trees and all other life forms.

9. Relax and allow the qualities of the Golden Era of Atlantis, such as levitation, teleportation, telekinesis and the telepathic sending of healing, to return to you.

The Third Eye Chakra

1. Focus on your third eye chakra and call in Archangel Raphael to open it and light it up into a totally clear crystal ball.

2. Send light from here to the planetary third eye chakra in Afghanistan and visualize an ascension flame burning here.

3. Now imagine a link connecting your third eye chakra to Jupiter.

4. Take the energy higher and link to Jumbay, its ascended aspect, meaning 'hugeness' and 'expanded vision to include All That Is'.

5. Feel the higher vibration of Jumbay flow through you as you say the name to yourself three times: 'Jumbay. Jumbay. Jumbay.'

6. Sense the crystal-clear light showering you with cosmic abundance so that you are abundant in your physical, mental, emotional and spiritual life.

7. The light is also bringing in the codes and symbols to open you to huge amounts of wisdom, joy and expansion and this enables you to connect with the wisdom of golden Atlantis. Relax and absorb this light.

The Crown Chakra

1. Focus on your crown chakra and call in Archangel Jophiel to open it and light up the thousand crystals or petals of your crown.

2. Send light from here to the planetary crown chakra in Machu Picchu, Peru, and visualize an ascension flame burning there.

3. Now imagine a link connecting your crown chakra to Uranus.

4. Take the energy higher and link to Curonay, its ascended aspect.

5. Feel the higher vibration of Curonay flow through you as you say the name to yourself three times: 'Curonay. Curonay. Curonay.'

6. Sense the crystal-clear light pouring divine transformation into your crown, enabling you to open up to a higher level so that you bring in higher enlightenment.

7. Relax and absorb this light.

The Causal Chakra

1. Focus on your causal chakra and call in Archangel Christiel to open it and ignite the glorious pure white ball of peace.

2. Send light from here to the planetary causal chakra in Tibet and visualize an ascension flame burning there.

3. Now imagine a link connecting your causal chakra to the Moon, which has already ascended.

4. Feel the vibration of the Moon flow through you as you say it to yourself three times: 'Moon. Moon. Moon.'

5. Sense the shimmering white light holding all the higher Divine Feminine qualities, including compassion, love, togetherness, caring, empathy, nurturing and co-operation, down into your causal chakra. It is also enabling you to embrace a higher and wider perspective on situations. It empowers people to work together.

6. Relax and absorb this energy.

The Soul Star Chakra

1. Focus on your soul star chakra and call in Archangel Mariel to open and light up the high-frequency ball of magenta light.

2. Send light from here to the planetary soul star chakra in Agra, India, and visualize an ascension flame burning there.

3. Now imagine a link connecting your soul star chakra to Orion, which has ascended.

4. Feel the vibration of Orion flow through you as you say the name to yourself three times: 'Orion. Orion. Orion.'

5. Sense the magenta light holding all the keys and codes of cosmic wisdom pouring into your soul star chakra.

6. Relax and absorb this energy.

The Stellar Gateway

1. Focus on your Stellar Gateway chakra, the huge glowing golden orange ball of light above you, and call in Archangel Metatron to open and light it up.

2. Send light from here to the planetary Stellar Gateway in the Arctic and visualize an ascension flame burning there.

3. Now imagine a link connecting your Stellar Gateway chakra to Mars.

4. And then take the energy higher, to the ascended aspect of Mars, Nigellay.

5. Feel the higher vibration of Nigellay flow through you as you say the name to yourself three times: 'Nigellay. Nigellay. Nigellay.'

6. Sense the golden orange light filled with the divine masculine qualities of the peaceful warrior pouring onto you. Within you, it is enhancing courage, constructive action, strength with gentleness, inspirational leadership and the power to protect the weak.

7. Relax and absorb this light.

Become an Ambassador for Earth

If you wish to work intergalactically and become an ambassador for Earth:

1. Prepare a space where you can be relaxed and undisturbed. Light a candle if you can.

2. Sit quietly and breathe comfortably with the intention of becoming an ambassador for Earth.

3. Ground yourself by visualizing roots going from your feet deep into the Earth.

4. Ask Archangel Michael to place his deep blue cloak of protection around you.

5. Sense your glorious shimmering aura reaching right out to the stars.

6. Link into the rainbow light of Seraphina, the mighty Seraphim, and feel her light connect to you.

7. Link down to Hollow Earth as your golden roots extend into the diamond centre of the planet.

8. Imagine yourself tall, grounded and strong as you stand in your power as a being of the universe.

9. Ask Seraphina if you may serve as an ambassador for Earth during your sleep. Say, either to yourself or aloud:

    'Beloved Seraphim Seraphina, I ask and pray with all my heart and soul that I may serve you and the universe by becoming an ambassador for Earth.'

10. Your intentions are noted and blessings are now pouring onto you from the spiritual hierarchy. Relax and absorb them.

You can do this visualization as often as you wish.

Step 12

Building Your Crystalline Light Body

For the past aeons we have lived in carbon-based bodies, which operate at lower frequencies. This was so that we could understand the third dimension, with its polarities of dark and light, and experience the lower senses.

Most people on the ascension path are currently in the fourth dimension, the level at which their heart chakra opens and they fully accept they are on an eternal soul journey. Their cells can hold up to 79 per cent light.

At the Cosmic Moment on 21 December 2012 the new crystalline light body was activated in the etheric for all those who hold this level of light. It is a compound six-pointed crystalline merkabah. This looks like two pyramids overlapping to form a three-dimensional six-pointed star and holds our energy fields at a higher frequency.

This crystalline light body is the blueprint of the humans we will become in the new Golden Age. It will come into place for everyone who is fifth-dimensional or at the upper levels of the fourth dimension and those whose soul wishes them to participate in the new Golden Age.

The purpose of having a crystalline light body is that it can hold more light than a carbon-based one. Light contains the love, knowledge and wisdom of the universe.

Therefore, in order to build our crystalline light body we must be able to take in more light. This can be done in the following ways:

- Eat light, fresh, organic food.

- Drink pure water.

- Bless everything that enters your body.

- Exercise regularly and lightly.

- Do what brings you joy.

- Keep your home physically and energetically cleansed, light and happy.

- Breathe deeply and take time to meditate and connect with your Higher Self.

- Practise the ascension exercises in this book.

At our current stage we can hold more than 80 per cent of light in our cells, yet still inhabit a body of flesh. However, our planet has ascended and her harmonics are rapidly changing. Over the next 20 years, as this crystalline matrix is established within the Earth, we will start to notice physical changes in our body that will attune us to the planetary energies.

When the crystalline light body is in the process of activation, as many people are now experiencing, the physical body will not need so much food. Light, like sunshine, will be metabolized as a source of body fuel. We will also be able to tune in to and absorb the light of the Great Central Sun.

As we move further into these elevated energies, our physical body will expand into higher possibilities. Physically, we will change shape. We will develop the longer heads that they had in Atlantis and Egypt to hold the expanded brain and the energy of the causal chakra. We will become taller and thinner and more androgynous.

Then, when we work in the etheric, we will operate at the seventh-dimensional frequency. Our crystalline light body will be activated and completely managed by our 12 fifth-dimensional chakras. Then, as walking masters, we will have access to all the light we need to keep ourselves in prime health and condition.

In future years we will have a choice as to whether or not we wish to maintain a physical body while living and learning on Earth.

The Crystalline Light Body and the Ascension Process

An understanding of the crystalline light body is an important part of the ascension process. It focuses us on the actions we need to take to ascend, and where attention goes, energy flows.

To have full access to the powers available in this new light body, we have to undergo the ascension process first – in other words, the cells of our body must hold at least 80 per cent of our possible light quotient. The instant the amount of light held in our cells reaches this level, we have ascended. For this to happen, our 12 chakras must spin at a faster frequency and all be in perfect harmony and alignment.

Once ascension has occurred, we will be expected to be fully responsible for our own healing and maintenance. Our auras will become much bigger, sometimes reaching up to 32 kilometres (20 miles), and on occasion surrounding the world.

When our energy fields expand, we will have to be very vigilant about keeping them clear, pure and protected, because we will be sharing energetic space with those who may be vibrating at a denser frequency. It will be up to us to look after our own energy systems.

However, every person who ascends will create a cellular chime within those around them and this will activate the light-body building process within them. So the ascension process will radiate outwards.

Building Your Light Body

1. Prepare a space where you can be relaxed and undisturbed. Light a candle if you can.

2. Sit quietly and breathe comfortably with the intention of building your light body.

3. Ground yourself by visualizing roots going from your feet deep into the Earth.

4. Ask Archangel Michael to place his deep blue cloak of protection around you.

5. Visualize yourself sitting in the centre of your crystalline merkabah, your personal six-pointed interlocking pyramids.

6. Ask Archangel Metatron to light this up for you at a seventh-dimensional frequency.

7. Then ask him to provide a column of pure light from the Great Central Sun and bring it down through your chakras into Hollow Earth.

8. Visualize it expanding to a 32-kilometre (20-mile) radius and lighting up.

9. See yourself glowing pure and clear like a crystal.

10. Ask your merkabah to anchor round you at a fifth-dimensional frequency.

11. Ask your Higher Self and Archangel Metatron to hold this at 80–85 per cent light quotient and adjust it according to your needs.

12. Thank Archangel Metatron.

Step 13

Light Dispensations

As the ascension process accelerates, Archangel Metatron is releasing bursts of specific light energy from the Great Pool of Atlantis, which recently merged with the Great Ascension Pool above the Pyramid of Giza. Together they create a mighty force.

At the fall of Atlantis the original pool was stored by Archangel Metatron and it has now been made available in limited bursts specifically for the ascension process. These very high-frequency concentrated releases of light enable us to move forward very quickly on our spiritual path by building our light body.

These 'light dispensations' also powerfully affect the establishment of our fifth-dimensional chakra column. When this light floods down from the Great Ascension Pool, it is received in the Stellar Gateway and moves down through the chakra column before it is anchored into Hollow Earth by Archangel Sandalphon. Calling in the energy of the Great Ascension Pool is a very effective method of permanently illuminating the fifth-dimensional crystalline light body.

During 2013 four specific light dispensations were authorized by Archangel Metatron and the Planetary Ascension Council based in Luxor. They were released in response to requests from human lightworkers and with each burst of light the magnitude of the energy increased. They harmonized with the light codes that are accelerating in frequency and with the many astrological alignments that made 2013 such a challenging year for those on the ascension path.

The first dispensation was in September 2013 and was specifically aimed at raising the percentage of light within the four-body system to 80 per cent.

The second dispensation, in October 2013, cleared etheric debris from the fifth-dimensional chakra column of those who were ready.

The third was in November 2013. This illuminated the fifth-dimensional chakra column and targeted the base and sacral chakras of those who were ready to fast-track their lessons.

The last dispensation of 2013 occurred on the winter solstice, 21 December, and the light codes released were much gentler and had the effect of calming and softening the process that everyone had been through during the year.

You can call for your own light dispensation by invoking Archangel Metatron and asking him to fill your four-body system with 80 per cent light. Ask him under the Law of Grace to provide a special light dispensation for this to take place. This will illuminate you with the frequency of an ascended master. Once this light is in your fields, it is your responsibility to focus on a place or situation that needs to be transmuted to a higher frequency.

From the start of 2014 the light that has been pouring out from the core of Helios has been of such intensity that no further light dispensations have been requested or needed. The integrations have been very intense and people are having to take in the energy while living their everyday lives. However, as more people become fifth-dimensional and are able to live with the higher frequencies, it will become appropriate for lightworkers to call in light dispensations once again to benefit all.

Dimensional Paradigms

There are three dimensional paradigms running concurrently on Earth at present. Masses of people are living out their third-dimensional reality. It is their soul choice to create and experience the conditions that are a reflection of their thoughts and beliefs. It is anticipated that before 2032 a light will go on in the collective conscious that will enable them to see life from a higher perspective. They will then open their hearts and souls to the fourth dimension. This sudden shift will accelerate the entire planetary ascension process.

In the meantime the fourth-dimensional paradigm has been fully activated as an energetic grid round the planet. We are now a fourth-dimensional planet and people worldwide are starting to develop a social conscience. This is also a deeply constructive period where the energy is reflected back from our thought processes almost instantly. Those on the spiritual path are now expected to use this time to build the fifth-dimensional reality that we are aiming for.

There are many who are living in the fifth-dimensional paradigm now by maintaining a spiritual attitude and focus. Thoughts create reality and this point of focus is providing lightworkers with a massive advantage as they strive towards the ultimate goal of ascension.

Invoking Archangel Metatron's Light

Here is a simple and very effective way to invoke Archangel Metatron's light from the Ascension Pool:

1. Prepare yourself for meditation.

2. Sit quietly and visualize a place or situation that needs pure ascension light. This can be anywhere of your choice.

3. Invoke Archangel Metatron to access the Ascension Pool, and ask him to dispense this pure light to your chosen area.

4. See golden orange light pour out from the mighty pool above the Great Pyramid of Giza.

5. Visualize and assist Archangel Metatron to direct the flow of light to where it is needed.

6.   Link hands with Archangel Metatron and hold the area in the highest integrity.

7.   See all sentient beings touched by the light – happy, joyous and filled with unity consciousness.

8.   Bless their ascension pathway and pour your own heart love into the flow of energy.

9.   Thank Archangel Metatron for the light dispensation.

10. Open your eyes and know that you have touched many lives for the highest good of all.

Step 14

The Law of Gratitude and Blessings

Earth is the accelerated learning plane of the universe and a life on Earth offers the greatest opportunity for spiritual growth that is available anywhere. Souls literally queue up for a chance to come here.

The first souls to take physical bodies at the start of Atlantis were in awe of all they were offered. Although they had gone through the Veil of Amnesia, they were incredibly grateful for their lives. They gave thanks for food, for pure flowing water, for being able to touch a tree and feel its texture and energetic imprint. They were grateful for the joy and sorrow of emotions. How amazing to smell a flower! How wonderful to taste fruit! Awe, delight and joy are all forms of gratitude. And the more thankful these souls were for life on Earth, the more good things were showered on them.

However, as they reincarnated again and again, Earth became familiar and they forgot the wonders of life, so they became denser and more distant from Source.

Every thought or energy we send out creates an etheric symbol. Certain radiant energies form such perfect geometric shapes that they act as keys to open doors of universal abundance. Gratitude and blessings are two of these radiant energies. So are other higher ascension qualities like faith, unconditional love and trust.

When the sacred geometry of our thought is a perfect match for the divine thought, the universe responds with an outpouring of abundance in alignment with our soul's desire.

As above, so below. If a child glows with pleasure when we give them a present, our heart expands with pleasure and we want to shower more gifts on them. The sacred geometry of their joyous response matches the frequency of our giving heart. However, when they expect gifts as a right, the geometry no longer matches, so we stop giving.

The universal response is similar. When we are grateful for something, more of that good thing comes to us. So, if for example you have a small garden and would like a bigger one, make what you have as beautiful as possible. Appreciate every tiny bit of it. That is the sure way of attracting a bigger one from the universe. You have shown you deserve it and are grateful.

If you would like to do more interesting work, put your heart and soul into the tasks you are given. Your enthusiasm will light up your aura and draw in work that brings you soul satisfaction.

If you would be glad of greater prosperity, appreciate every single thing you can afford. Say thanks for every pound in your bank account. Your gratitude magnetizes more.

You get a new job. You have a baby. You buy a house. How do you respond? Are you ready to open your heart and say, 'Thank you, I'll do my very best'? Responsibility is a gift that offers you the opportunity to respond to the universe. It is a chance to show gratitude.

Genuine gratitude is an abundance tool. Be grateful for all that you have and more will flow to you.

There are two archangels who can assist you to expand your chakras so that you are able to feel genuine appreciation. Ask Archangel Chamuel to expand your heart so that you really can give heartfelt thanks for your experiences. Ask Archangel Gabriel to raise the frequency of your base and sacral chakras to the fifth dimension, for it is when you feel safe, secure and trusting that you are ready to give genuine thanks for all you have.

A Gratitude Walk

A gratitude walk is a simple and effective way of opening your eyes to the awesome and totally free gifts that surround you. You can do this as a physical walk or as a visualization.

A Gratitude Walk Visualization

1. Prepare a space where you can be relaxed and undisturbed. Light a candle if you can.

2. Sit quietly and breathe comfortably with the intention of taking an inner gratitude walk.

3. Ground yourself by visualizing roots going from your feet deep into the Earth.

4. Ask Archangel Michael to place his deep blue cloak of protection around you.

5. Invoke Archangel Chamuel to touch your heart.

6. Set off on a relaxed, safe walk along a beautiful sun-drenched path.

7. A stranger passes and you exchange a smile. Offer inner gratitude.

8. A bird is sitting on a branch singing his heart out. Listen with all your attention.

9. A dog barks. What is it trying to communicate?

10. You run your hand through flowing water. Enjoy the flow of love of the universe.

11. Feel the grass under your feet and tune in to the song of the Earth.

12. Touch a tree and wonder at the feel of the bark. Be aware of the tree roots forming a network round the planet and add love to it.

13. Look at the sky and be in awe at the vastness of the cosmos.

14. Take as much time as you like to experience and enjoy the wonders of nature.

Gratitude for Material Things

Here you can offer gratitude for tangible things in your life that make everyday existence more pleasurable, e.g. car, house, etc.

1. Prepare a space where you can be relaxed and undisturbed. Light a candle if you can.
2. Sit quietly and breathe comfortably with the intention of really appreciating your material blessings.
3. Ground yourself by visualizing roots going from your feet deep into the Earth.
4. Ask Archangel Michael to place his deep blue cloak of protection around you.
5. Invoke Archangel Gabriel to place his fifth-dimensional diamond in your base and sacral chakras.
6. Turn on a tap and be grateful for clean water.
7. Give thanks for the food in your cupboards.
8. Give thanks for your friends and family.
9. Give thanks for your home.
10. Give thanks for what you do have in your bank account.
11. Name every good thing in your life.

Blessings

The Law of Blessings works in a very similar way to the Law of Gratitude. You must have your heart open to receive or give blessings. When you bless from your heart, there is an energetic impact on the recipient. When you genuinely wish someone well and open your heart to them, a golden light containing geometric symbols of love flows from you to them. These symbols overlay and dissolve something within the other person and set them free. They also light up your own heart.

When you generously, open-heartedly bless someone who has hurt or harmed you, incredible divine alchemy takes place. The golden energy you have sent out dissolves your pain and also the third-dimensional energies in the other person. These blessings are some of the greatest ascension gifts you can give.

If someone has hurt or harmed you, start by intending to forgive them. Then call on Archangels Chamuel and Gabriel to help your blessings become totally heartfelt. Gradually, they will be.

If someone injures you financially, bless them with prosperity and picture money flowing to them. Archangel Gabriel will ensure that the money you lost is returned to you multiplied, possibly from another source.

If someone damages your property, tune in to the underlying cause within them. Then bless them with self-love, self-esteem, love or abundance and anything you feel they need for soul happiness. Visualize them receiving what they need. Put passion into the vision you send until you sense that they accept love and goodwill in their hearts. You will feel better. Your light will be brighter. And something will change within them.

When you bless others with qualities of grace, the codes of love within these qualities ignite the latent possibilities within those people. Blessing is a route to peace on Earth.

When you are ready to bless someone who has hurt you or your loved ones, you have achieved the ultimate sacrifice of ego, a mighty step on the ascension path. The perpetrator harmonically feels your mercy and their aura is lit with unconditional love. They receive a blast of love to the heart that may open them to ascension. You ascend to higher levels of spiritual growth and feel a deeper sense of peace.

Because consciousness spreads by harmonic transference, you also spread healing and grace to people you meet.

A Blessing

1. Ask Archangel Chamuel to bless your heart. Sense it opening.

2. Ask Archangel Gabriel to bless your soul. Feel it expanding.

3. Bless trees with happiness.

4. Bless flowers and plants with vitality.

5. Bless animals with love.

6. Bless warmongers with peace.

7. Bless sick people with vibrant health.

8. Bless places where people dump their litter or lower energies with divine peace and love.

9. Bless lonely people with friendship.

10. Bless the poor with prosperity.

11. Bless world leaders with integrity.

Step 15

The Ascension Path of Love and Kindness

There are many paths to ascension, but the one that transcends them all with its simplicity is the path of love and kindness. It is the basic foundation for every path and the angels of love, peace and joy will enfold us to enable us to maintain the qualities we need. The Buddha consciousness, the consciousness of the peaceful spiritual warrior, illuminates this pathway.

There are those who live simple lives, who have never heard the word 'ascension' or even of archangels, yet they ascend gloriously. Many of these are walking the path of love and kindness. Sometimes they live in impoverished communities, where they generously and joyfully share all they have. Some have large families and happily go without in order to feed their offspring and enfold them with love. Others go out into the world and selflessly serve those less fortunate. When these open-hearted people pass over, their friends and family usually say, 'They would have given their last penny to help others' or 'They would have done anything for anyone.'

Here are some of the qualities that we can cultivate as a foundation for this path: love, kindness, courtesy, warmth, listening from the heart, graciousness, generosity, openness and trust. These are all based on love consciousness and abundance consciousness.

The key to living this path is to ask ourselves, 'How would I behave if I were an angel?' This is the path that develops our etheric wings, which are radiations of light from our heart centre.

Love Consciousness
We have love consciousness when all the petals of our heart are fully open. We truly believe that everyone deserves to be loved and cared for. We accept everyone exactly as they are. We carry within us the Divine Feminine light, which automatically enables us to listen to, care for and empathize with others and respond to all people and situations with kindness and wisdom. We understand oneness.

Abundance Consciousness
We have mastered abundance consciousness when we totally trust that our needs will be met by the universe. We are then in a state of flow, knowing that there are never gaps in the stream of plenty. In fact, when we live in abundance consciousness, all that we freely give away comes back to us multiplied. We truly share and co-operate in all things. Our heart radiates generosity of spirit and wealth. These qualities are the essentials of the fifth-dimensional communities that will be created in the new Golden Age.

How to Develop These Qualities
God and his angels do not just give us these qualities. Rather, they send us people and situations that enable us to practise love and kindness.

If we need to practise generosity, they will place on our path people in need. Will we open our heart and give or will we close it and withhold? Will we use discernment and discrimination or will we give without due consideration? Once we are ready or have set the intention to walk this path, chances to test ourselves will be available.

Every single time we choose to respond to someone kindly, graciously, courteously or sensibly, it is lighting up this path a little more. If we practise and develop qualities of love, warmth, decency, honesty or generosity, our light will shine beautifully.

Ascension through Caring

Before we come into this world, our Higher Self and the Higher Selves of our entire family, along with our guides and angels, choose the life conditions of the family members. Some of these may relate to caring for others. There are people who devote their whole lives to the loving care of disabled relatives, for example. Occasionally this is a karmic situation, but increasingly the sick one, at a soul level, is offering to serve the ascension growth of the carer.

Alzheimer's Disease

There are many reasons for a person to develop this dis-ease. It may be karmic. It may be a decision to withdraw from the responsibilities of life. It may be to experience living from the heart, not the head. However, it may be to offer a carer or family member the opportunity to practise love and kindness.

Boundaries

When we are caring for others while walking the path of love and kindness, it often means that we have to be very clear about our boundaries. We must send out energy and act in a way that means we are treated with respect and honour, and remain true to ourselves while keeping our heart warm and open.

This is the ascension path of the peaceful spiritual warrior, the Buddha consciousness. Remember to ask Archangel Gabriel to give you clarity and the spiritual discipline to walk your path honourably.

Visualization for the Path of Love and Kindness

You can invoke Archangel Chamuel to keep your heart open at the most challenging times. When you are on this path, the angels of love and peace are always near you, pouring their ineffable love over you.

1. Prepare a space where you can be relaxed and undisturbed. Light a candle if you can.
2. Sit quietly and breathe comfortably with the intention of walking the ascension path of love and kindness.
3. Ground yourself by visualizing roots going from your feet deep into the Earth.
4. Ask Archangel Michael to place his deep blue cloak of protection around you.
5. Place your hand on your heart and invoke the angels of love and peace.
6. Sense them enfolding you in beautiful soft golden light.
7. Invoke Archangel Gabriel and ask him to help you find clarity about your path and your boundaries and the spiritual discipline to walk your path honourably.
8. Feel Archangel Chamuel strengthening the golden centre of your heart.
9. Be aware of your boundaries and your divine magnificence.
10. Visualize a person who is challenging you.
11. Look into their eyes and understand their underlying pain.
12. Respond with love and kindness.
13. Look again into their eyes. What do you see there now?
14. If you see fear, repeat the visualization as often as you need to. When you see a loving response, your energy truly has been one of love and kindness.
15. Thank the angels and open your eyes.

Step 16

The Path of Acceptance, Forgiveness and Harmlessness

Acceptance, forgiveness and harmlessness are angelic qualities and are an integral aspect of the Christ Buddha consciousness. This is a blending and amplifying of the two energies of Christ consciousness and the Buddha consciousness. These are the primary qualities of unconditional love. When we are on the ascension path, they must be offered to all sentient beings throughout the universe for, as part of the ascension process, we are required to integrate and manifest these open-hearted qualities.

They are also the essential core of fifth-dimension life in the new Golden Age that we are all moving into, and when everyone embraces them, there will be world peace and inner joy. When this occurs, everyone will enjoy a sense of confidence and self-worth and animals and humans will be in harmony with each other. This idyll is approaching! The more we practise living these qualities and envision this golden future, the more quickly it will manifest.

Acceptance
Acceptance literally means recognizing and accommodating all sentient beings exactly as they are without judgement or expectation. When we are accepted, we feel valued and therefore safe to be open about ourselves. As we feel free to

express our soul qualities, we blossom. Our aura expands, as there are no secrets or feelings to hide.

When acceptance is enjoyed within families, it sets all the members free to be themselves. This has a magical effect, as everyone feels secure. The same applies to countries and cultures. Where people are embraced and included exactly as they are, happiness results.

As personal, family and ancestral karma is now being swept away in the tide of high-frequency energy flowing into the planet, the old is dissolving and being replaced by genuine love and acceptance.

Acceptance is a function of all the chakras, but particularly the sacral chakra. Pink light is now flowing from Lakumay, the ascended aspect of Sirius, into the sacral chakras of those who are ready. This is healing old energies at a deep level.

A simple exercise you can do to bring yourself into acceptance and harmony is to ask Archangel Gabriel to place the diamond blueprint of your fifth-dimensional sacral chakra into your abdomen.

Forgiveness

One of the greatest tests while we are in a human body is unconditional love. In order to pass this test, we have to practise forgiveness. It can help if we understand that no one can do anything to us unless at a soul level or at some subconscious level we have agreed to it.

Also, while in a human body, we have only part of the picture. Our brave and beautiful loving soul, operating from a higher perspective, sets up the tests to see if we are ready to overcome the challenges and ascend.

Very often we find it hard to forgive because the pattern of abuse we are suffering has been set up in other lives and runs very deep. But holding on to old thoughts and emotions can distort the energy flow in any of the seven third-dimensional chakras, and forgiveness sets us free. It heals us physically, mentally, emotionally and spiritually. It is an act of self-love that releases our spirit to fly. It enables us to see things from a different perspective.

It is time now to dissolve the old so that the fifth-dimensional chakra column can descend fully. Here is a very powerful forgiveness prayer which Diana originally wrote for her book *Discover Atlantis*.

❖ *Forgiveness Affirmation* ❖

I forgive everyone who has ever hurt or harmed me, consciously or unconsciously, in this lifetime or any other, in this universe, dimension, plane or level of existence or any other.

I offer them grace.

I ask forgiveness for everything I have ever done to hurt or harm another, consciously or unconsciously, in this lifetime or any other, in this universe, dimension, plane or level of existence or any other.

I ask for grace.

I forgive myself for everything I have ever done to hurt or harm another, consciously or unconsciously, in this lifetime or any other, in this universe, dimension, plane or level of existence or any other.

I accept grace.

I am free. All chains and restrictions fall from me. I stand in my full power as a master.

Harmlessness

Harmlessness is the true route to total safety on Earth. When our aura is completely at peace and we are one with everyone, we are harmless. We radiate this around us so every person or creature we meet senses it and feels safe with us. Peace attracts peace. Harmlessness attracts love.

No one can enter our aura with lower intent unless we allow it through our fear or lack of self-belief. However, if you are a very high-frequency being who wishes to offer someone an opportunity to experience your grace, your soul may allow such a person to enter your aura.

Birds and animals flocked round St Francis of Assisi because he radiated harmlessness and they knew they were safe. Animals can read the aura and are good indicators of the energy a person is emanating. In the Golden Era of Atlantis all animals, birds, trees and plants were harmless. They developed defensive methods only when the frequency devolved.

You can ask Archangel Gabriel to help you to experience true harmlessness by placing the diamond blueprint of your fifth-dimensional chakra into your base centre.

When your fifth-dimensional blueprint overlays your third-dimensional one, the higher frequencies automatically raise the lower ones to perfection. So here is an exercise to help you on your journey to acceptance, forgiveness and harmlessness.

Visualization for Acceptance, Forgiveness and Harmlessness

1. Find a place where you can be quiet and undistributed.

2. Ground yourself by visualizing roots going down from your feet deep into the Earth.

3. Invoke Archangels Gabriel, Uriel, Chamuel, Michael, Raphael and Jophiel.

4. Tell them that you wish to bring the qualities of acceptance, forgiveness and harmlessness into your seven third-dimensional chakras.

5. Ask Archangel Jophiel to place the fifth-dimensional template of your crown chakra into place, blazing with the qualities of acceptance, forgiveness and harmlessness.

6. Ask Archangel Raphael to place the fifth-dimensional template of your third eye chakra into place, blazing with the qualities of acceptance, forgiveness and harmlessness.

7. Ask Archangel Michael to place the fifth-dimensional template of your throat chakra into place, blazing with the qualities of acceptance, forgiveness and harmlessness

8. Ask Archangel Chamuel to place the fifth-dimensional template of your heart chakra into place, blazing with the qualities of acceptance, forgiveness and harmlessness.

9. Ask Archangel Uriel to place the fifth-dimensional template of your solar plexus chakra into place, blazing with the qualities of acceptance, forgiveness and harmlessness.

10. Ask Archangel Gabriel to place the fifth-dimensional template of your sacral chakra into place, blazing with the qualities of acceptance, forgiveness and harmlessness.

11. Ask Archangel Gabriel to place the fifth-dimensional template of your base chakra into place, blazing with the qualities of acceptance, forgiveness and harmlessness.

12. As your seven chakras light up, see them descending into the Earth.

13. Bring down the 12 chakras in your fifth-dimensional chakra column.

14. Finally call on the unicorns to pour their light into your 12 fifth-dimensional chakras until they become one column of unified light.

15. Visualize yourself acting with true grace and harmlessness.

Step 17

Source Love Within

When your original divine spark, your Monad or I AM Presence, left Source, it was gifted a ball of energy that contained angel light and Source love at the 12th-dimensional level. This high-frequency ball of love and light is still held within your Monad.

And then it was the turn of your Monad to send out aspects of itself. It sent out 144 extensions. These are souls, who operate at a slower frequency. The ball of angel light and Source love was stepped down to a seventh-dimensional level and was encoded within each soul. Some of these souls are the Higher Selves of incarnated humans.

Earth is a very special place. In order to incarnate here your soul must be at least seventh-dimensional, so all beings on Earth have angel light in their souls. It is at birth or during early childhood that most people close down their connection to their Higher Selves.

When you reach the upper levels of the fifth dimension, your merkabah merges with your soul energy. This means that as long as you maintain the higher levels of the fifth dimension you have angel energy and divine love within your fields. At this point you can access the angel light within.

At the third, fourth and lower spectrum of the fifth dimension, you must call in the angels to assist and protect you. As you take upper fifth-dimensional mastery, you command your own angel energy to do your higher will and protect you. At this point you can access deep blue Archangel Michael energy from within yourself and radiate it for strength and protection. You can summon up your inner Archangel Gabriel light for clarity and purification. You can call on your Archangel Raphael aspect for healing or abundance, or Archangel Jophiel for wisdom, or Archangel Uriel for empowerment, or any other angel or archangel energy to bring light from your inner core to serve your highest good.

When the relevant archangelic energies are anchored and spinning at a fast frequency within your 12 chakras, your light becomes very bright. You can also anchor other archangels into your fields. For example, if you are connected to animals, you can call on your inner Archangel Fhelyai. His divine codes within your energy fields will be able to support, comfort or protect animals who are in your presence. Your thought forms will also contain the archangel codes, which you can then project to the animals.

When you are connected to your inner archangels in this way, you become a radiant, glorious master and light being.

Visualization to Connect with Your Inner Archangels

Here is an exercise to help you re-anchor the archangels into your chakras or energy fields. We suggest you call in the fire dragons first to transmute any lower vibrations within you.

Your chakras are like interconnecting cogs. As soon as one starts to spin more quickly, the others must do so too. We suggest you work from your base to your Stellar Gateway. When these 11 wheels are ready, place below them your Earth Star chakra containing Archangel Sandalphon's energy. Then activate the Earth Star with sound and all your chakras will rotate exponentially faster. You will become a beacon of light!

1. Prepare a space where you can be relaxed and undisturbed. Light a candle if you can.

2. Sit quietly and breathe comfortably with the intention of connecting to Source and to angel light within you.

3. Ground yourself by visualizing roots going from your feet deep into the Earth.

4. Ask Archangel Michael to place his deep blue cloak of protection around you.

5. Call in your fire dragons and ask them to place a wall of fire round you. Then ask them to send a burst of fire up your chakra column from your Earth Star chakra, transmuting any lower energy.

6. Focus on your base chakra and invoke Archangel Gabriel. Sense his pure white light filling your chakra and being anchored there. Then allow this chakra gradually to turn platinum.

7. Focus on your sacral chakra and invoke Archangel Gabriel. Sense his pure white light filling your chakra and being anchored there. Then allow this chakra gradually to turn luminous pink.

8. Focus on your navel chakra and invoke Archangel Gabriel. Sense his pure white light filling your chakra and being anchored there. Then allow this chakra gradually to turn vibrant orange.

9. Focus on your solar plexus chakra and invoke Archangel Uriel. Sense his golden light filling your chakra and being anchored there. Then allow this chakra gradually to become deep gold.

10. Focus on your heart chakra and invoke Archangel Chamuel. Sense his pink light filling your chakra and being anchored there. Then allow this chakra gradually to turn white with a hint of pink.

11. Focus on your throat chakra and invoke Archangel Michael. Sense his deep blue light filling your chakra and being anchored there. Then allow this chakra to radiate deep blue.

12. Focus on your third eye chakra and invoke Archangel Raphael. Sense his emerald light filling your chakra and being anchored there. Then allow this chakra gradually to become clear like a crystal ball.

13. Focus on your crown chakra and invoke Archangel Jophiel. Sense his yellow light filling your chakra and being anchored there. Then allow this chakra gradually to turn crystal clear.

14. Focus on your causal chakra and invoke Archangel Christiel. Sense his pure white light filling your chakra and being anchored there. Then allow this chakra to radiate white.

15. Focus on your soul star chakra and invoke Archangel Mariel. Sense his magenta light filling your chakra and being anchored there. Then allow this chakra to radiate magenta.

16. Focus on your Stellar Gateway chakra and invoke Archangel Metatron. Sense his golden orange light filling your chakra and being anchored there. Then allow this chakra to radiate golden orange.

17. Now turn your attention to your Earth Star chakra and invoke Archangel Sandalphon. Sense his silver-grey light filling your chakra and being anchored there. Then allow this chakra to radiate silver-grey.

18. To activate the Earth Star chakra, hum a deep note into the chakra.

19. Sense it starting to spin very fast at a fifth-dimensional frequency, so that all the other chakra cogs in the column spin at this frequency too.

20. As you become a beacon of fifth-dimensional light, tone, sing or hum all your chakras into harmony.

You can focus on any other angels or archangels as well. When you name them, they will start to engage in your energy fields and the spin of your 12 chakras will enable their frequency to fully anchor there.

A Ball of Outer Archangels

A way of accessing your outer archangels easily is by placing yourself in an archangel ball. This is very simple. Here is an exercise to make one.

Making an Archangel Ball

1. Prepare a space where you can be relaxed and undisturbed. Light a candle if you can.

2. Sit quietly and breathe comfortably with the intention of surrounding yourself in an archangel ball.

3. Ground yourself by visualizing roots going from your feet deep into the Earth.

4. Ask Archangel Michael to place his deep blue cloak of protection around you.

5. Imagine a ball of light forming round you.

6. Call Archangel Michael into the front section and see his deep blue fill this area, bringing you strength, courage and protection.

7. Call Archangel Uriel into the section on your right and see his golden yellow fill this area, bringing you confidence, self-worth and self-empowerment.

8. Call Archangel Gabriel into the section behind you and see his pure white light fill this area, bringing you purity, clarity and joy.

9. Call Archangel Raphael into the section on your left and see his emerald light fill this area, bringing you healing and abundance.

10. Call Archangel Sandalphon into the section below your feet and see his silver-grey (or black-and-white) light fill this area, keeping you grounded and enabling you to fulfil your potential.

11. Call Archangel Metatron into the section above your head and see his golden orange light fill this area, illuminating you like a Sun.

12. Invoke the Gold Ray of Christ to fill the centre of the ball with golden light. Or you can invoke Archangel Chamuel to fill the centre with pink love or Archangel Mary to fill the centre with turquoise Divine Feminine light.

13. You can call other archangels into this ball if you wish.

14. Now relax and bathe in this beautiful and empowering archangel light.

Step 18

The Lunar Influence

The celestial beauty of the Moon has been worshipped for aeons and lunar energy is incredibly powerful and affects every living being on this planet. As well as being responsible for tidal flows and personal energy cycles, the Moon has a deep and penetrating influence on our current ascension process. It takes the Sun's masculine energy and reflects it to Earth as a beautiful Divine Feminine frequency. Since the Cosmic Moment on 21 December 2012, more and more Divine Feminine energy has been flowing from the Moon, illuminating the DNA within us all as we start to ascend.

During the Golden Era of Atlantis, masculine and feminine energies were perfectly in balance. When that civilization fell, masculine energy began to predominate. Men took control everywhere and disempowered women. At a spiritual level, women allowed this.

The masculine side of humanity is left-brain and logical. The traditional male role is to be strong and protective, find food for the family and go out hunting, and therefore the male has a wider picture of the area in which he finds himself than the female. So, metaphysically, the masculine expands horizons, takes ideas, carries them through and seeks knowledge. The left brain works with technology and science and develops communications. When masculine energy becomes excessive, the social structure becomes power-based, acquisitive, hierarchical and aggressive. It needs to be balanced with creative, loving feminine energy.

The feminine side is right-brain, creative and spiritually connected. The traditional female role is to create a home, conceive babies, care for the family and nurture it, so wisdom, compassion, loyalty, responsibility to the race, intuition and receptivity are feminine qualities. Metaphysically, the feminine conceives new ideas and looks after them until they are ready to come to fruition. When society is overbalanced on the feminine side, this leads to stagnation and inertia, so that people do not develop their potential. This needs to be balanced with clear-thinking, decisive, action-based masculine energy.

Currently, lunar energy is lighting up the right brain of everyone on Earth in order to develop the feminine qualities in us all. When these are accepted, and more individuals and cultures develop masculine and feminine qualities equally, a sense of peace and safety will pervade the planet. When the masculine and feminine work together in divine harmony, creative ideas and spiritual technology will be born and developed in a perfect way.

Lady Luna, the master of the Moon, is currently taking many people and societies through initiations into the feminine aspect, so that they can truly express qualities like harmlessness, unconditional love and peace.

One of the most powerful lunar influences of recent years has been the Moon's task of reflecting and magnifying the codes of Helios, the Great Central Sun, that stream through our own Sun. These light codes are received into our cells to illuminate the DNA that has been dormant since the fall of Atlantis. We are receiving this intense reprogramming day and night, and will continue to do so until we have harmonized with the higher crystalline matrix of Gaia.

A supermoon is a new or full Moon that closely coincides with the Moon's closest point to Earth in its orbit. Supermoons appear bigger and brighter than the average Moon and cause larger than usual tides. They dynamically affect the cells of our body as they bathe them, and the DNA they contain, in the light of the Silver Ray.

Since 2012 the number of supermoons has increased. There were five in 2014. They are particularly influential when they correspond to significant astrological alignments. For example, the supermoons around the time of the April 2014 Grand Cardinal Cross magnified and intensified the Divine Feminine light pouring onto Earth and all sentient beings and accelerating change.

The extremely powerful full Moon of 18 August 2014 fully ignited the flow of Christ consciousness within the waters of our planet. It also activated the Aquarian Ascension Pool, a pool of energy formed in Atlantis and now held at a ninth-dimensional frequency, so that its energy could be taken, upgraded and distributed to areas of need.

As the ascension of our planet accelerates towards the new Golden Age, we are promised that the Moon will flood us with transcendent love from the higher portals of the Cosmic Heart.

As well as carrying the highest and purest Christ Light, Archangel Christiel spreads his energy via the Moon. He returned to serve Earth when people started to open their fifth-dimensional causal chakras. In fact the causal chakra, when activated, looks like our own personal celestial body just above our head.

We can connect with Archangel Christiel very easily when the Moon is waxing. He has also taken over the upkeep of the Aquarian Ascension Pool. When this energy is invoked, it is stepped down from the ninth dimension via the Moon to become accessible at a fifth-dimensional level.

Visualization to Connect to Lunar Energies

If you have a piece of moonstone, keep it with you during the day. Hold it in your left hand as often as possible to enable it to connect to the energy systems of your entire body.

1. Prepare for meditation by grounding and protecting yourself.

2. Visualize yourself under a beautiful full Moon and invoke the mighty Archangel Christiel.

3. Feel the illumined lunar white presence of Archangel Christiel filling your aura and your fields.

4. He is taking your hand and leading you along a bright white moonlit pathway towards a magnificent building with pure white walls. It is taller than the eye can see.

5. Archangel Christiel invites you to enter this Mansion of the Moon and you step inside. Soft white drapes and ornate light structures flow before your eyes. The ceiling, far above your head, has a portal directly in the centre.

6. You sit below this opening and moonlight comes flooding down on you, so that you are in a glowing circle of pure lunar energy.

7. Feel this calm Divine Feminine light filling every cell of your body.

8. See it lighting up your mental, emotional and spiritual bodies too, until you are utterly filled with this energy.

9. Feel every part of yourself coming into perfect balance, your masculine and feminine energies blending and unifying into oneness, the Christ consciousness.

10. Ask this light to activate the DNA within your cells. Visualize the codons within the strands coming to life, sparkling with ascension light.

11. Send this beautiful light to an area that needs balancing. Ask Archangel Christiel's angels to illuminate the dense energies there and to sing over them.

12. It is time to leave the Mansion of the Moon with Archangel Christiel. Thank him and the Moon for their loving gifts.

13. Open your eyes and carry the pure light of the Divine Feminine out into your life.

Step 19

Archangel Sandalphon

Archangel Sandalphon is known as the tall angel, because his energy is said to reach up to the heavens. He is the twin flame of Archangel Metatron, the alpha and the omega. His colours are black and white, but he is often seen as grey or silver, which is the perfect blend of the two shades. This frequency carries psychic awareness and spirituality. Archangel Sandalphon's symbol is the black and white yin/yang symbol, representing the perfect balance of masculine and feminine energy.

In order to bring us fully into harmony with our divine blueprint, Archangel Sandalphon presents our prayers to Source, along with his added energy.

Archangel Sandalphon and the Earth Star Chakra

Archangel Sandalphon is in charge of the development of the Earth Star chakra, currently the most important chakra, as it is the foundation for the people we are to become, the ascended root race of the sixth Golden Age on Earth.

The year 2032 marks the start of the sixth Golden Age. By then our planet must be restructured so that humans and animals can also physically change their cells into a crystalline form. This will mean that we can literally hold more light, and glow. Then we will be ready to develop new spiritual technology and access extra-terrestrial wisdom and assistance from the angelic realms. Currently spiritual technology is ready and waiting for us to draw in the templates that will allow it into manifestation.

Archangel Sandalphon's etheric retreat is the magic crystal cave at the beautiful blue Lake Atitlán in Guatemala. Here we can access his wisdom and work with him to activate our Earth Star chakra. This must be fully activated to form a solid ascension base for the 12 fifth-dimensional chakras we are now developing. Below our feet, it is our own personal Garden of Eden, holding the seeds of our potential and our joy. Archangel Sandalphon nurtures this chakra and helps it to develop when we are ready. When it is activated, our Stellar Gateway to Source can open and in addition we can connect to the seventh-dimensional centre of the planet, Hollow Earth.

Kundalini is the vital or life force energy. For 10,000 years the kundalini of the planet has been held in the Gobi Desert by ascended master Sanat Kumara as a masculine energy. In 2008 the Mayan elders moved it to Archangel Sandalphon's retreat in South America, where he transformed it by divine alchemy into a feminine energy. The whole of South America is connected to Venus and has the Divine Feminine within its essence, so here the ball of kundalini was imbued with the love energy of the Cosmic Heart. The kundalini of our planet is now a Divine Feminine blueprint contained in our Earth Star chakras. This will be the basis for the ascension transformation for everyone in the new Golden Age. When it rises within an individual, the ascension process truly starts.

London, UK, is the Earth Star chakra of the entire planet. The waking of the 12 fifth-dimensional chakras of the planet in 2012 lit up the grids on Earth and connected the feminine kundalini to London. So, Divine Feminine energy is contained in the ascended aspect of London.

Call on Archangel Sandalphon to ground you into the seventh-dimensional diamond core of Hollow Earth as well as into your fifth-dimensional body. When you have done this, it completes the Antakarana bridge, the energetic bridge running through you all the way to Source.

The Angel of Music

Because of his understanding of the harmonics of creation, Archangel Sandalphon is known as the angel of music, and he works with Fekorm, the great master of music, who has joined us from another universe to help Earth through this transition to the new Golden Age. They will enable us to connect with the Music of the Spheres, the divinely perfect harmonies created by the movements of the celestial bodies. This will raise our frequency so that we can each access our individual divine fifth-dimensional blueprints.

Archangel Sandalphon's perfect balance of masculine and feminine energy also demonstrates that he is grounding us in a completely balanced way, enabling us to be in total harmony and flow. When this is fully integrated, the music emitted by our vibration will create harmonics that will bring us into total peace.

Archangel Sandalphon's Fifth-Dimensional Bubble

You can call on this mighty archangel to place a fifth-dimensional bubble over you and this will bring your entire energy field into the higher frequency. In fact when you ask him to do this, he places your own Earth Star Chakra over and around you, anchoring it below your feet. This enables all your chakras to align in the fifth dimension and opens up the higher potential of each centre.

This is a very powerful thing to do. You should only ask Sandalphon to do this for someone else if they expressly ask you to do so, for if their energies rise too quickly they can feel ungrounded, irritable or even ill.

You can, however, ask Archangel Sandalphon's angels to stand at the gate of your home or by your front door and place his fifth-dimensional bubble over everyone who enters. This will raise the frequency of all visitors for a few moments. It can enable them to see things differently or to change their mind if they have entered with lower intent.

Visualization to Receive Archangel Sandalphon's Fifth-Dimensional Bubble

1. Prepare a space where you can be relaxed and undisturbed. Light a candle if you can.

2. Sit quietly and breathe comfortably with the intention of receiving Archangel Sandalphon's fifth-dimensional bubble and connecting to the note of your divine blueprint.

3. Ground yourself by visualizing roots going from your feet deep into the Earth.

4. Ask Archangel Michael to place his deep blue cloak of protection around you.

5. Ask Archangel Sandalphon to activate your Earth Star chakra until you can see it shimmering silver-grey below you.

6. Ask him to guide the fifth-dimensional bubble up from your Earth Star right over your energy fields. Your aura is now silver and reflective.

7. Take a moment to feel this resonance through every cell of your body, your aura and your fields.

8. Feel yourself grounded and connected to the heart of Mother Earth. Then sense her energy flowing into you and expanding your bubble.

9. Imagine you are standing on your two feet and visualize your bubble starting to expand and spread out.

10. See it going out through your street, your country, across the oceans and finally encompassing the entire planet.

11. Feel the musical vibrational resonance of every sentient being merging with yours. You are at one with your planet.

12. Now you can access the note of your perfect divine blueprint. Relax and let it chime in every cell of your body.

13. Thank Archangel Sandalphon and open your eyes.

Step 20

Archangel Gabriel

Archangel Gabriel is a pure white source of archangel energy, for white contains all spectrums. He represents the higher form of purity held within the hearts of humanity.

Currently Archangel Gabriel is overseeing the purification of the planet as well as that of all sentient beings here. He is in charge of the element of fire, holding the pure White Flame to bring everything through the transmutation of fire to the highest possible frequency. While he works in co-operation with the unicorns of air, Lady Gaia of earth and Poseidon of water, it is he who holds the clear blueprint for the level of light that is envisioned for the planet. If you aspire to higher ascension, you can invoke Archangel Gabriel to assist you with the clearance of your own density and that of the planet.

Archangel Gabriel's twin flame is Archangel Hope. She is the rainbow within the facets of the diamond, bringing new opportunities and inspiration. When you see a rainbow and your heart leaps with joy, she opens new doors for you to enable your path to shine with light.

Archangel Gabriel and the Base, Sacral and Navel Chakras

Archangel Gabriel is in charge of the development of the base, sacral and navel chakras for humanity and those of the planet.

The Base Chakra

The fifth-dimensional base chakra is platinum and when we reach this frequency our life is grounded in shimmering bliss and joy, based on total trust that the universe will provide for us. Currently, blockages in the base chakra are hindering the ascension process of many people because they are influenced by the collective consciousness about money and power. This needs to be raised. If we ask Archangel Gabriel to do so, he will assist with the clearance of our base chakra. However, he may send us a lesson to help us with this clearance!

The planetary base chakra is in the mountains of northern China and we can help the world by visualizing Archangel Gabriel's pure white diamond of light over this area.

There is a symbiotic connection between the chakras of the planet and those of humanity and when enough individuals clear their base chakras, the planetary base chakra in China will light up and vice versa, so we can make a difference.

The Sacral Chakra

The sacral chakra of the planet is in Honolulu. At a fifth-dimension level it is a beautiful pale iridescent pink, full of transcendent love.

Because of the return of the fifth-dimensional energies, individuals in partnerships that are not serving their highest good are being given the opportunity to separate or move into a higher frequency. Many relationships are being transformed and many twin flame or soul-mate relationships are being reactivated.

When we have completed the wheel of karma, we have the opportunity to make pre-life choices with love and grace – and this will start to transform family life. We can then call on Archangel Gabriel to purify our family karma, so that our family is set free.

When we raise our frequency to the higher fifth dimension, our physical body must vibrate with pure health. As the vibration of our sacral chakra rises, Archangel Gabriel is bringing forward the fifth-dimensional blueprint for perfect radiant sexual and emotional health within us. We can call on him to accelerate this – but should be aware that a lesson may present itself in the process.

We can also ask Archangel Gabriel to help raise the vibration of this chakra in humanity.

The Navel Chakra

In the Golden Era of Atlantis everyone had a separate navel and sacral chakra. However, as the fifth-dimensional chakras withdrew and were replaced by third-dimensional ones, the two chakras merged. They are now separating again.

The navel chakra is magnificent bright orange and is the colour of planetary unification. When it is fully fifth-dimensional and gloriously radiant, we will welcome each other and all cultures and religions with total acceptance, as we will have integrated the planetary Christ consciousness.

This is when fifth-dimensional communities and golden cities will emerge. There will be no boundaries or passports. We will see the divine in each other. We will live as one. Call on Archangel Gabriel to help you hold this vision for humanity.

Simplicity

Simplicity is divine. The truth is always clear, precise and shining. Archangel Gabriel can help us to pinpoint the simplicity of truth. Situations and lessons in life are often more obvious than they initially appear. Furthermore, if we do things for the highest good of all, Archangel Gabriel will ensure that a simple solution that suits everyone will evolve. He holds the mirror of truth to show us the most effortless way to live our life.

The Diamond of Clarity

If you are not clear about your next step in life or you have to make a choice or take a decision, sit quietly and ask Archangel

Gabriel to bring you clarity. He will clear any clutter around a situation so that you can see the higher perspective or he may send a sign or bring an opportunity.

As the Veils of Illusion have started to lift, people's thoughts have become more muddled because of the merging of past-life memories and emotions yet to be acknowledged, resolved and dissolved. This is called parallel bleed-through and it can be very confusing when these thoughts and emotions come to you. Archangel Gabriel can separate these for you and place a diamond of clarity over you. All you have to do is ask.

Archangel Gabriel's Etheric Retreat

Archangel Gabriel's retreat is above Mount Shasta, the beautiful and pure snow-tipped mountain in the Cascades in northern California. Here you can access his purity, clarity and wisdom and work with him to activate and clear your base, sacral and navel chakras.

Etherically, his retreat resembles a diamond. If you wish to visit it during your sleep, ask his angels to collect you and take you there in your spirit body to receive the clarity, purification or higher light that you need. It is also helpful to think about Archangel Gabriel during the day, which will help you to attune your vibration to his so that you are ready for your night appointment.

If you wish to visit to his retreat during meditation, here is a suggested visualization:

Visualization to Visit Archangel Gabriel's Retreat

1. Prepare a space where you can be relaxed and undisturbed. Light a candle if you can.

2. Sit quietly and breathe comfortably with the intention of visiting Archangel Gabriel's etheric retreat.

3. Ground yourself by visualizing roots going from your feet deep into the Earth.

4. Ask Archangel Michael to place his deep blue cloak of protection around you.

5. Ask Archangel Gabriel to place a pure diamond of clarity over your energy fields to hold you in the highest light.

6. Ask him to activate and spin out anticlockwise any red energy within your base chakra. Then spin in clockwise brilliant platinum light.

7. Visualize your life filled with bliss and joy.

8. Ask him to activate and spin out anticlockwise any dense murky energy within your sacral chakra. Then spin in clockwise glorious pink transcendent love.

9. Visualize everyone on the planet in vibrant health and all families worldwide bonded in love and unity.

10. Ask Archangel Gabriel to activate the full radiance of your navel chakra.

11. Visualize yourself walking joyfully hand in hand with Archangel Gabriel along your golden ascension path.

12. Ask Archangel Gabriel to expand the diamond around you to encompass the entire world.

13. Now you can ask his angels to take you to his retreat:

    'Beloved Archangel Gabriel, I ask and entreat that you send your pure white angels to conduct me to your etheric retreat.'

14. If you have a specific request, make it now.

15. Relax deeply and visualize yourself being taken up into a vast shimmering cosmic diamond above Mount Shasta.

16. Rest here as long as you need to, then thank Archangel Gabriel and return to where you started.

Step 21

Archangel Uriel

Archangel Uriel, who radiates the most glorious deep gold of wisdom, is working tirelessly to dissolve lower frequencies and release humanity into freedom and happiness. Whenever it is karmically appropriate, he visits pockets of dense energy and transmutes them, carrying them to Source to be dissolved. Call upon him when situations become difficult.

He also holds within his vast energy fields a ruby red light. This intervenes, when directed, to terminate situations that have exceeded their creative potential for good. Whenever possible, he intercedes for peace.

When we connect to the Ruby Ray, we become a channel for Archangel Uriel. The ruby is the physical form of this ray. The Ruby Ray contains purple, which consists of red, royal blue and gold. Royal blue gives us the power to communicate a depth of wisdom and knowledge. Archangel Uriel can transfer his light through this colour to us with a boost of energy that enables us to absorb it.

Soft gold contains ancient wisdom and this can be accessed when our centre is peaceful and serene.

Red gives us the physical strength and stamina to hold this level of power and communicate it to others. It gives the energy and impulse for action.

Archangel Uriel's twin flame is Archangel Aurora. She has the energy of the dawn light that illuminates ideas and

inspires new beginnings. She is currently making her frequency available to those lightworkers who are bringing in important new information from spirit, assisting them with its verification. She gives us confidence in our ability to connect with spirit and also ensures that all the information provided comes from a point of oneness.

Archangel Uriel and the Solar Plexus Chakra

Our solar plexus draws in any fear that is around us. It is our alarm system, like a huge psychic pump watching out for us. It takes in the lower energy of fear and tries to transmute it.

All gut reactions are felt within the solar plexus. Currently most high-level psychics who download important information from the spiritual realms verify the truth of it through their solar plexus. Archangel Uriel is now assisting them to raise their frequency to the heart and verification will in future come as warmth in the heart chakra. Our golden wisdom then forms the core of our heart centre.

South Africa is the solar plexus of our planet. It absorbs the third-dimensional fear for the entire world and transmutes it. When a solar plexus is in perfect harmony, it vibrates to the note B. During the World Cup held in South Africa, the people were creating the note B with their vuvuzelas in order to transmute the fear and tension of the world. This was organized by Archangel Uriel.

Our planet is the solar plexus of the universe and also vibrates to the note B. We absorb the lower energies for the entire universe, which is why there has been so much stress here. Now, while the old is being released, Archangel Uriel is holding the blueprint for the higher manifestation of world peace. World peace will arise freely when people have high personal satisfaction and self-worth because they will be aligned to their soul path.

When you are ready to come into harmony and balance, call on Archangel Uriel to help you to understand what has been preventing it and to dissolve it. Your deepest wisdom will

then automatically emerge from within you to guide you to the highest outcome for the situation presented.

Within our fifth-dimensional solar plexus we hold the knowledge and wisdom of our entire soul journey from when we left Source. As we integrate more and more closely with Archangel Uriel, we automatically start to access this again. The symbol within the third-dimensional solar plexus chakra is the six-pointed star, the bringing of Earth to Heaven and Heaven to Earth. At the fifth-dimensional level, all the chakras contain Christ consciousness, so the symbol becomes an illumined multi-dimensional six-pointed star. When we visualize this in our solar plexus, we activate the light codes of our wisdom.

Earth has had a very long journey and earned much wisdom through five Golden Ages. This is all stored within the etheric diamond pyramid at the centre of Hollow Earth. As our solar plexus is cleared, we can enter the pyramid and access the Akashic records for Earth. We are also able to access all the wisdom acquired throughout our soul journey in this and other universes. The level of information that we receive is triggered by our personal frequency.

The fifth-dimensional solar plexus chakra reflects the deep gold of Archangel Uriel's divine power, wisdom and commitment to bringing about new beginnings in alignment with the Divine Feminine. These are the qualities upon which the fifth-dimensional communities will be founded.

Archangel Uriel used to work with communities in the Golden Era of Atlantis. He would bring people together and inspire in them the ability to work co-operatively with each other for the highest good.

Angels of Peace

Archangel Uriel commands a host of Angels of Peace. You can call on him to send them anywhere, wherever they are needed for individual or country situations or for planetary assistance. Each Angel of Peace is so vast that it can enfold you or overlight an entire city. You may see these angels in any colour frequency from creamy gold to ruby gold. You can be of huge assistance to people as well as the world by mentally or verbally sending them to people and places in need. Do this as often as you can and remember that, unless you send them, they are unemployed.

The dove is a symbol of the Angels of Peace and you can visualize this flying wherever its light is required. However, the Angels of Peace also work through ducks, pigeons, partridges and pheasants. When one of these birds approaches you, the Angels of Peace have sent it, so pause for a moment and fill your heart with peace. Archangel Uriel will be close to you.

Archangel Uriel's Retreat

Archangel Uriel's etheric retreat is in the Tatra Mountains of Poland. Here you can access his light to help you connect with your original wisdom and to strengthen your solar plexus chakra. His retreat resembles a vast golden ruby-tinted rose that is glowing, warm and welcoming, like the Sun. If you wish to visit him here in your spirit body during your sleep, prepare yourself during the day by thinking about him and visualizing yourself surrounded by a shimmering golden ruby colour. When you go to bed, ask his angels to conduct you to his retreat to be soaked in peace so that your true wisdom can emerge.

If you wish to connect with him during meditation, here is a visualization:

Visualization with Archangel Uriel

1. Prepare a space where you can be relaxed and undisturbed. Light a candle if you can.

2. Sit quietly and breathe comfortably with the intention of visiting Archangel Uriel's etheric retreat.

3. Ground yourself by visualizing roots going from your feet deep into the Earth.

4. Ask Archangel Michael to place his deep blue cloak of protection around you.

5. Focus on your solar plexus and see it as a huge golden rose with ruby-tipped petals.

6. Invoke Archangel Uriel with the words:

   'Mighty Archangel Uriel, I ask you to enfold me in your golden cloak, lined with ruby light.'

7. Sense his energy enfolding you and pouring into your solar plexus, so that the petals open wide.

8. Breathe the red, royal blue and gold of his Ruby Ray gently in and out of your solar plexus.

9. Be aware it is strengthening you so that you stand in your power and magnificence.

10. Sense the great stream of knowledge and wisdom of all your soul's journey and of Earth herself waiting to be revealed in your life.

11. Quietly send Angels of Peace to people and places that they are needed and know this is making a difference.

12. Ask Archangel Uriel's golden angels to take you to his etheric retreat while you sleep.

13. Thank Archangel Uriel and know that you will always have a connection with him.

Step 22

Opening the Heart with Archangel Chamuel

Opening the heart chakra is the most important step on the ascension path, for working from this core centre brings us clearly into the higher fifth-dimensional paradigm.

The heart is represented by a beautiful pink-and-white rose with a golden centre. The first section of the heart has 10 petals. Each of these is an initiation of the third dimension. They take the form of qualities that we must overcome and are rigorously tested by our guides and our Higher Selves. It is possible to open the higher petals of the heart and still have lower petals closed. This happens if a lesson is yet to be learned in the base or sacral chakra.

The second section of the heart, which takes us through the fourth dimension, has seven petals or initiations, and these lessons are usually learned more quickly.

The fifth-dimensional section of the heart has 16 petals as we open to the higher heart and finally to transcendent love. (For more information see *Ascension Through Orbs* by Diana Cooper and Kathy Crosswell.)

Working through the heart transcends the ego, for everything is done for the highest good and resonates with unity consciousness. When enough people operate via their heart centre, balanced with left-brain reasoning and with the purest intention, fifth-dimensional societies will emerge. Everyone within them will be heart-centred and do what they love to do.

Opening the 33 petals of the heart is the journey of the soul as it discovers and explores all aspects of love on its adventure back to Source. This usually takes several lifetimes, but in the rarefied energy of this era people are being presented with the opportunity to explore all the petals as they undergo the ascension process.

Archangel Chamuel is overseeing the opening of the first 10 petals and the early ascension initiation process. Many people, even though they are moving quickly along the ascension path, still have the third-dimensional blueprint of their issues contained within the cellular matrix of their heart chakra. This means they may still be tested by some of the lower emotions.

We understand that one way to help these petals to open and release the emotional strain is to invoke Archangel Metatron and visualize his golden orange Sun pouring down into your heart. This automatically enables your rose to open and to bring the emotions to the light.

Where the upper levels of your petals are awaiting activation, you can call on Archangel Mary to bathe them in her transcendent love frequency. This softens them and encourages them to open.

These fifth-dimensional facets of the petals of the higher heart chakra are as follows:

- Forgiveness of the entire Earth experience which is a residue from the fall of Atlantis. This can be healed by calling in the golden Christ Light and sending it back to that point in time in Atlantis. This will reset the planetary matrix at that point and allow us all to move forward.

- Forgiveness of self is so much more difficult than forgiveness of others. This is because we really know at some deep level the magnificence of our own soul. If you place the Cosmic Diamond Violet Flame over yourself frequently, this will enable you to reconnect with your own divine magnificence. Sit quietly and invoke the Cosmic

Diamond Violet Flame. Visualize and feel yourself drenched in pure crystalline violet light. When you have done so, it will totally release your disappointment with yourself for not being perfect.

- Warm-heartedness is an automatic process that occurs as the heart opens to a fifth-dimensional frequency. The ascension journey melts the ice of previous experiences and allows the Christ Light to flood in. When you visualize the ice around your heart melting and the Christ Light flowing in, you facilitate this.

- As soon as your heart glows with love, you feel open and welcoming to all sentient beings. Consciously picture your heart chakra glowing and send this light to all beings.

- Generosity is the gift of your heart to others. This may be symbolized by material giving. When you give anything, however small or large, make sure your heart is open.

- Unconditional giving, when you give freely to others without any thought of return, is a reflection of the openness of your heart. Practise this and you will soon feel your heart becoming warm.

- Love for humanity comes from complete acceptance of all souls, no matter what stage of learning they are at. Bless all people, whatever they seem to have done.

- Unconditional love is a pure outpouring of love without conditions. Notice how free the love is that you offer. If you notice a limitation in your love, ask Archangel Chamuel to dissolve it.

- Transcendent love takes all lower frequencies and through the power of divine alchemy brings them to Source. Visualize your love creating a cellular chime of love within others, then demonstrate by giving pure love to a person or situation that has tested you.

- Connection with the Cosmic Heart is part of our divine blueprint. We are always bringing through aspects of this. However it is only when we transcend lower aspects of the heart that this manifests in our everyday life. Call in the ninth-dimensional aspect of Archangel Chamuel and ask him to connect you to the Great Cosmic Rose, the Cosmic Heart.

- Cosmic love is the flow of love of the universe that passes through our physical body to encompass all that is. If you can, go out under the stars and breathe love from all of them into your heart, then send love back to them.

- Oneness is the complete identification with Source and the deep knowing that we are part of it and it is part of us. Imagine yourself blending with every atom of the universe. You are All That Is.

Harmonizing the Heart

The cosmic symbol that is held within the heart is the circle or the yin/yang symbol. These two symbols are interchangeable and they balance the flow of energy through the 12 chakras. Symbols were chosen in ancient times because of the effect that the shapes have on the flow. This is something that cannot be learned but must be experienced.

Visualization to Harmonize the Flow of Energy within the Heart Chakra

1. Sense or visualize a circle or the yin/yang symbol in your heart chakra.

2. Move your attention up to the Cosmic Heart and allow love from there to flow into your Stellar Gateway chakra, then down through all your chakras, round the ball in your heart centre and down into the Earth Star.

3. Then repeat this as the energy flows up from your Earth Star, round the ball in your heart chakra and up to your Stellar Gateway again.

Archangel Chamuel

Archangel Chamuel has been looking after the heart centres of humanity since the fall of Atlantis and understands us well.

His Divine Feminine aspect is Archangel Charity. She represents the open-hearted giving aspect of Chamuel's light and inspires people to act selflessly. Her colour is radiant white with a beautiful hint of pink.

Archangel Chamuel's etheric retreat is in St Louis, Missouri. There is a vast bed of quartz crystal underneath this state in the south of the USA. This is why Archangel Chamuel created his retreat in the etheric above this place. At the Cosmic Moment on 21 December 2012 this crystal bed was activated in alignment with the planetary harmonics to raise the frequency of the entire planet and this is enabling Archangel Chamuel's love energy to spread.

You can visit Archangel Chamuel's retreat to access his pure love energy and open and expand your heart. If you wish to visit in your spirit body during sleep, take time in the day to visualize your heart being connected to Chamuel's heart by a beautiful pink cord. If you wish to visit him in meditation, here is a visualization you can practise:

Visualization to Visit Archangel Chamuel's Retreat

1. Prepare a space where you can be relaxed and undisturbed. Light a candle if you can.

2. Sit quietly and breathe comfortably with the intention of visiting Archangel Chamuel's retreat.

3. Ground yourself by visualizing roots going from your feet deep into the Earth.

4. Ask Archangel Michael to place his deep blue cloak of protection around you.

5. Imagine there is a beautiful pink-and-white rose in your heart.

6. Breathe gently in and out of your rose and see the 33 petals starting to open as you relax.

7. Ask Archangel Chamuel to touch your heart chakra. You may sense this or feel a glow from your heart.

8. Ask Archangel Metatron to pour his golden orange light, like glorious sunlight, onto your heart. As the petals absorb the rays, sense them surrendering any third-dimensional aspects still within you.

9. Ask Archangel Mary to pour her clear light of pure love over your higher heart and sense these petals opening wide in the transcendent light.

10. When all the petals of your rose are fully open, be aware of the central core glowing gold.

11. Receive a ray of light from the Cosmic Heart filled with the codes and keys of Source love.

12. Feel yourself being surrounded by Archangel Chamuel's angels as they take you to his retreat.

13. Relax and absorb love.

14. Thank Archangels Chamuel, Metatron and Mary before opening your eyes.

Step 23

Archangel Michael

Archangel Michael is the best-known figure in the archangelic realms. Since the dawn of humanity he has inspired souls to live at a higher level by beaming strength, courage and truth into them. He has tirelessly protected the frequency of human beings on this planet and this has been very necessary while we have been living on a plane of duality. His task now is to illuminate us at a fifth-dimensional level. As this happens, our belief systems will transform. Then we will be able to protect ourselves with our own inner power.

Archangel Michael is overlighting Canada and North America and is responsible for the angelic light that he has placed strategically in the ground throughout these countries. This light is positioned within the grids and is specifically programmed to illuminate the web of light round the planet in a harmonious way. This will accelerate the rate at which we wake up spiritually.

In the glorious fifth-dimensional reality, the new frequency will fully support our belief in self-sufficiency. We will know that we are safe at all times, protected by our inner light.

As we develop our personal power, Archangel Michael will always be there to shield us. When our light is strong enough and we trust and believe we are safe, we will be.

Archangel Michael's Sword of Truth represents the inspiration to stand in our own power, speak our truth and lead others forward into the blazing light of their own magnificence. At a fifth-dimensional level we are self-reliant and consciously generating our own reality. Then we hold our own Sword of Truth.

Archangel Michael now stands with us, empowering us. As we have raised our own frequencies, his higher energies can now be perceived as a lighter vibration of the same colour. So they are no longer deep blue but royal blue, containing the red energy that we need to help us take action for the light. He is currently helping us to bring our throat chakras into a higher frequency where we can be totally honest. When 75 per cent of humanity does this, the great wave of awareness will push us all into the fifth dimension. Michael will then empower the leaders of the future to set up the fifth-dimensional structures that will take us into the Golden Age.

Every one of us has incarnated with certain levels of strength and courage that we have earned during our lifetimes. Archangel Michael is helping us manifest these in our everyday life by rebalancing and restructuring our energy fields. As soon as he sees that we are ready, he presents us with the tests we need to bring these energies fully into our consciousness. Then he leads us onto our path of Christ consciousness, carrying his Sword of Truth.

Archangel Michael is an incredible alchemist and mathematician who works with the geometric structures of all dimensions. His influence spreads throughout all the universes. He co-operates with Archangel Metatron. Together they create sacred geometric structures infused with the light language that contains specific sounds, and this solidifies matter into reality. This is how these archangels enable physical manifestation to take place. It is how new stars and planets are created. It also applies to the powerful thought-forms we send out that create our reality.

Archangel Metatron provides the Helios Source Codes that are the keys of life. These energies from the Sun are activating us now. So, Archangel Metatron takes the thoughts of Source as well as our powerful thoughts and desires and projects them into the reality of our world. Then Archangel Michael solidifies the geometry of this into living matter.

Commander Ashtar is in charge of the Intergalactic Fleet that patrols Earth and the outer rim of our galaxy. The fleet protects this space to enable the flow of light from Source to continue freely through to our planet. Commander Ashtar therefore works closely with Archangel Michael, whose forces are ensuring the uninterrupted ascension process of Earth.

Because Archangel Michael is holding an aspect of the fifth-dimensional blueprint whereby power and control are replaced by unified love, sharing and co-operation, he is also enabling new business structures to arise on Earth. We are already seeing his influence in the collapsing of the old paradigm within the economy, business, pharmaceuticals, schooling, healthcare, industry and government as we move into the new paradigm.

Archangel Michael's twin flame is Archangel Faith. When you connect with her energy she gives you such clarity of purpose and utter trust that you feel supported and know all is in divine order.

As we manifest the wishes of our Higher Self, the archangel energy within us becomes apparent in our life. We carry within us Archangel Michael's qualities of strength and courage, as well as the energy of the peaceful warrior of love, the true leader of vision and power, who helps and protects all those striving to live at a higher level.

Archangel Michael and the Throat Chakra

Archangel Michael is in charge of the throat chakras of all sentient beings. As our throat chakra radiates the wonderful royal blue of the fifth dimension, we start to connect to the wisdom of Mercury and its ascended aspect, Telephony. Then we can access wisdom from the Golden Era of Atlantis. In addition we will communicate with angels and masters on the

Gold Ray, which carries the Christ Light of unconditional love as well as the wisdom of the universe, and have a telepathic connection with all species of animals and extra-terrestrial beings. When we can communicate with animals, this will enrich our life and enable the animals to be on their own ascension path with more freedom.

Through the Gold Ray, we will receive downloads into our throat chakra that will enable us to communicate the language of light, which carries the ascension information for the world. Furthermore, we will be able to feel the energy of the angels.

As we connect with the wisdom of the Golden Era of Atlantis, Archangel Michael will oversee the facets of information that become available to us. He will enable us to spread this with courage to those who are ready for it, which will boost our ability to speak our truth.

Archangel Michael's Retreat

Archangel Michael's retreat is in Banff, Canada, over the sacred blue Lake Louise in the mountains. If you visit him here, he will illuminate you with his strength and power so that your can protect yourself. You can fully open your throat chakra to your truth and he will place your own Sword of Truth in your energy fields.

If you wish to visit his retreat in your spirit body when you are asleep, imagine yourself immersed in deep blue light and act at all times with strength and courage.

If you wish to visit his retreat during meditation, here is a visualization you can use:

Visualization to Visit Archangel Michael's Retreat

1. Prepare a space where you can be relaxed and undisturbed. Light a candle if you can.

2. Sit quietly and breathe comfortably with the intention of connecting to Archangel Michael.

3. Ground yourself by visualizing roots going from your feet deep into the Earth.

4. Ask Archangel Michael to place his deep blue cloak of protection around you and surround yourself in royal blue light.

5. He is taking you through the dimensions to an etheric castle shimmering with sapphire and gold light.

6. Here he invites you to sit on a royal-blue throne.

7. Feel your throat chakra opening up and radiating royal blue light.

8. Be aware of this energy from your throat connecting to Mercury and its ascended aspect, Telephony. You receive a download of wisdom from the Golden Era of Atlantis.

9. Feel yourself surrounded by the blazing golden light of angels and Masters of the Gold Ray.

10. Relax and listen to any communications.

11. Tune in to an animal and telepathically send it love, gratitude and freedom.

12. Archangel Michael hands you his Sword of Truth, radiating a shining white light tinted with crystal blue.

13. Relax here to absorb his light and his teachings.

14. Thank Archangel Michael.

Step 24

Archangel Raphael

Archangel Raphael is guiding us to co-create the perfect vision of fifth-dimensional oneness and abundance. He oversees the abundance consciousness of humanity. For aeons we have looked to an outside source, such as nature or God, to provide our livelihood. Now, however, Archangel Raphael is teaching us that our source of abundance is infinite and is entirely dependent on our own personal beliefs. When our frequency matches the vibration of our expectations and this is in alignment with our Higher Self, our dreams will automatically be fulfilled.

The faster our frequency, the more quickly we are able to manifest these dreams. Due to the acceleration in the frequency of our planet, our manifestation process is at least 10 times faster than it was at the turn of the century. Archangel Raphael is drawing our attention to the speed at which we are able to create our new reality. Any thought, positive or negative, is reflected back in physical form if sent out with enough drive. Weak thought-forms are held within our aura and our energy fields and can affect our health. Golden angelic thoughts create a golden aura and vibrant health.

Archangel Raphael and the Third Eye Chakra

Archangel Raphael is also responsible for the massive amount of work taking place in the third eyes of people at present.

At the lower levels of the fifth dimension, this centre glows with pale green crystal light and as we move into the higher aspects it becomes a clear crystal ball of enlightenment.

As a general principle, the clearer and more open this chakra becomes, the more our gift of clairvoyance returns to us. As it is clears, we are also able to see our own magnificence and connect with the angelic frequencies more easily.

The third eye is a powerful tool that is used for manifestation in all dimensions. This is where we see our vision and send out the thoughts that bring the vibration into our life in physical form. It is one of the most important tools in our ascension process and must always be used with the highest intent.

When our third eye chakra is fifth-dimensional, we can send a connection out to Jupiter and its ascended aspect, Jumbay. When we beam the vision we wish to create up to Jumbay, it is blessed by this mighty planetary consciousness. Then it is bounced back to our etheric energy field to be solidified the moment we are ready. When we focus a clear, disciplined mind on our vision, miracles take place immediately.

When we enjoy cosmic abundance consciousness, this reflects in our personal prosperity. Archangel Raphael is teaching the principles of abundance and manifestation so that we can stand on our own two feet as masters. We can provide everything for ourselves when our consciousness is attuned to the higher possibilities.

The fifth-dimensional third eye chakra of this planet is Afghanistan and when enough people bring their own third eye into clarity and enlightenment, that country will automatically reflect this by restoring peace. In the new Golden Age, Afghanistan will be a majestic fifth-dimensional location.

Health and Happiness

Archangels Raphael and Mary are twin flames. They hold the divine blueprint for the perfect health and happiness of humanity.

Archangel Raphael overlights any form of healing in this universe and is with anyone who is giving healing, whether it is hands-on, distance, counselling, massage or any other form of healing on the physical or etheric level. He is also with the person receiving healing.

You can call on Archangel Raphael to assist with the healing process of your own body and its etheric structures or those of other people. The Law of Non-interference states, however, that you do not interfere with another person's lessons. When you ask Archangel Raphael to give or send healing, he will only work under the Law of Grace. This means that healing will only take place with the permission of the Higher Self of the person involved and for the highest good of all.

This mighty archangel also co-operates with the Lords of Karma, so that when they bring our karma forward, he surrounds us and heals it.

Within the fifth-dimensional blueprint all the chakras are clear and flowing, so the body radiates a healthy cellular structure. Currently in the collective consciousness there is a belief that the physical body is limited in its powers to regenerate after certain injuries. In truth the only thing that limits a physical body is the belief structure of the individual. Every cell of our body responds directly to the power of our thoughts, so the fifth-dimensional blueprint supports a perfect physical sheath.

Some souls choose to incarnate into a damaged body to balance karma, but now most do so in order to give others lessons in unconditional love and acceptance or to challenge and expand the beliefs held in the collective consciousness.

While any angelic being of the seventh dimension or above can heal, call in Archangels Raphael or Mary to bring the fifth-dimensional blueprint into alignment.

Archangel Raphael also works with the unicorns to help bring about enlightenment for individuals and humanity. He works on the Emerald Ray and the emerald gemstone is the physical manifestation of his presence on Earth. His energy helped to co-create the Emerald Tablets, brought through by Thoth in ancient Egypt.

On a third-dimensional level, the Emerald Tablets speak of wisdom and the journey of humanity through darkness striving for the light. There is a facet of these Tablets that remains untranslated until we reach a unified level of consciousness. Then we will be capable of understanding the language of unconditional love, the Christ Light that reached perfection in the Golden Era of Atlantis. This light was placed within the layers of the Emerald Tablets by Archangels Raphael, Michael and Metatron, as well as Thoth, to be released as Earth ascends to its new peak.

Archangel Raphael's retreat is in Fatima, Portugal. We can visit him here to receive healing and tune in to cosmic abundance and enlightenment. We can also work with him in the following visualizations:

Working with Archangel Raphael for Abundance

1. Prepare yourself for this visualization by relaxing into a meditative state.

2. Visualize or sense yourself cocooned within a giant emerald.

3. Imagine your third eye is a crystal ball and breathe into it.

4. Decide what you want to manifest for the highest good.

5. Send this picture to Jumbay and visualize it being empowered with the cosmic light of creation.

6. Picture your beautiful vision becoming solid.

7. Fully expect it to manifest in your life.

Working with Archangel Raphael for Enlightenment

1. Prepare yourself for this visualization.
2. Sense or feel Archangel Raphael's hand on your third eye. It is illuminating the crystal ball in your third eye.
3. Think of a situation in your personal life or the world.
4. Allow a picture of the higher perspective of this to form in your crystal ball.
5. Ask Archangel Raphael to hold this vision in its angelic frequency.
6. Know that each time you do this you are expanding your levels of enlightenment and practising high-level manifestation.

Working with Archangel Raphael for Healing

1. Prepare yourself for this visualization.
2. Feel every cell of your body vibrating with emerald green light.
3. Have a sense of this manifesting perfect fifth-dimensional health in your body.
4. See yourself glowing with health and vitality.
5. Ask Archangel Raphael to send blessings of healing to all those you love and then to all those in need.
6. Visualize his emerald green healing light flowing to a person or animal who needs it for the highest good.
7. Send Archangel Raphael's light round Earth to heal our beautiful planet.

Step 25

Archangel Jophiel

Archangel Jophiel helps us to connect to our wisdom and cosmic knowledge and also to spread it to others. His twin flame is Archangel Christine, the Divine Feminine aspect, who carries the Christ Light.

Archangel Jophiel and the Crown Chakra

During the ascension process, Archangel Jophiel is responsible for the development of the fifth-dimensional crown chakra of every being in the universe.

Archangel Metatron sends each individual soul on Earth a download of light, depending on their level of spiritual progress. Contained within this are the codes to their ascension process. Light contains spiritual information and knowledge. Wisdom is the ability to apply that knowledge for the highest good of all. Archangel Jophiel oversees the activation of the data contained within the light codes received during this process. He then helps each soul to translate this information through their crown chakra. This enables us to work with the energy of Source in everyday life.

At the third-dimensional frequency, the crown chakra is pale yellow, while in the fifth dimension it becomes a shimmering clear crystal with a hint of gold, the Gold Ray of Christ.

The crown chakra contains 1,000 petals, which is why it is known as the thousand-petalled lotus. Each petal contains a code of our personal wisdom for our ascension pathway. In addition a thread from each one connects directly to other parts of the cosmos, such as a planet or great energy. Archangel Jophiel triggers these when we are ready. He co-operates with other archangels or the unicorns to do this. When our crown is fully open, we are in touch with the entire universe and with Source.

When the petals are open, two things happen. First the links from the cosmos through our Monad into our crown create geometric formations. They light up so that we are seen by the Powers That Be as a master in the universe. Our progress is then monitored tirelessly by the angelic team that is responsible for us.

Secondly, these open petals form a bowl to accept the cosmic light of knowledge and wisdom being brought through the transcendent chakras. They then pass it down our body to the other chakras in acceptable amounts.

All cosmic input enters the body through the crown. It is then filtered and distributed by the third eye. Here Archangel Raphael helps us to expand our levels of enlightened awareness so that our perception of the information remains true to the original impulse from Source.

While this activation is taking place within the crown and is spreading down into the third eye, it is very common to feel symptoms associated with the head, maybe tension headaches, a tender crown, blurred vision or tinnitus. The physical energies associated with these spiritual changes will cease as the high-frequency energy starts to descend and flow freely through the other chakras into our Earth Star.

For a full activation of this chakra, it is helpful to invoke both Archangel Jophiel and his twin flame Archangel Christine.

Where people are behaving unconsciously or without due consideration for others, Archangel Jophiel and his angels move into a position where they can pour wisdom onto them. If they accept this light, it enables them to make higher choices about

THE ARCHANGEL GUIDE TO ASCENSION

their attitudes and actions. If you feel that Jophiel's energy is needed, you can ask him to send his angels to a particular place. For example, if people are speeding down a residential road where children are vulnerable, you can ask Archangel Jophiel to watch over it, or you can send his energy to leaders of banks or industry who are behaving unwisely.

Education

Archangel Jophiel is holding the educational blueprint for the children of the future and also assisting teachers in schools. He is bringing in the new paradigm for the schooling of children and the further education of adults. In future children will be taught more as they were in the Golden Era of Atlantis. They will spend more time out in nature and playing games. They will learn the universal laws. Future education will honour and develop the needs, gifts and talents of each individual child so that their soul can feel satisfied and they can fulfil their fifth-dimensional blueprint.

Archangel Jophiel is also assisting the teachers on the planet who are bringing forward a knowledge of the ascension process to impart it to others. If you are drawn to work with him, you are on a teacher's path and may also be connected to Lord Kuthumi, the new World Teacher in the inner planes.

Archangel Jophiel's Retreat

Archangel Jophiel's etheric retreat is in the mountains in the north of China near the Great Wall. If you wish to link to his energy more closely, before you go to sleep ask his angels to take you to his etheric retreat in your spirit body. He will help you to connect with your wisdom and cosmic knowledge heritage as he and his angels light up the petals of your crown chakra. He will also inspire you to spread your knowledge and wisdom to others.

Here is a visualization you may follow if you wish to visit his retreat in meditation:

130

Visualization to Visit Archangel Jophiel's Retreat

1. Prepare a space where you can be relaxed and undisturbed. Light a candle if you can.

2. Sit quietly and breathe comfortably with the intention of visiting Archangel Jophiel's retreat.

3. Ground yourself by visualizing roots going from your feet deep into the Earth.

4. Ask Archangel Michael to place his deep blue cloak of protection around you.

5. Imagine yourself sitting in a golden lotus flower open like a chalice.

6. All the petals are open and sacred shapes are raining down on you, bathing you in their cosmic wisdom.

7. There is a magnificent pure white unicorn above you, lighting up and activating the shapes.

8. As each one is absorbed by your energy fields, your wisdom is enhanced.

9. Now invoke Archangel Jophiel's angels to conduct you to his etheric retreat.

10. Sense or feel the golden light of many of his angels surrounding you.

11. Find yourself in a cosmic golden chalice above the mountains of northern China.

12. Relax here and receive light from Archangel Jophiel.

13. When you are ready, thank Archangel Jophiel and feel your golden aura filled with wisdom and knowledge.

Step 26

Archangel Christiel

Archangel Christiel sends his frequency through the universe to us like a finger of God. When we need him, he steps through a cross-shaped diamond-white stargate in Lyra to reach the Pleiades, which act as a transformer for him down to a seventh-dimensional frequency. From here he accesses Earth through his retreat at Jerusalem. His twin flame, Archangel Mallory, has an etheric retreat over Bethlehem, through which he enters Earth. It was part of the divine plan that Jesus should bring the Christ energy through at this location on our planet, a place where it was already represented.

The Christ Light is a ninth-dimensional consciousness which would etherically burn us out if it shone onto us. Because of this, Archangel Christiel holds the blueprint for us at a seventh-dimensional level.

Archangel Christiel and the Causal Chakra

Archangel Christiel is in charge of the pure white causal chakra, which is above the crown, and his light, containing pure Christ Light, is poured into this chakra at a frequency that we can handle. Once the causal chakra is activated during the ascension process, we are permanently connected to this great universal angel.

When we first become fifth-dimensional, the causal chakra is slightly towards the back of the head, but at the upper levels of the fifth dimension it moves fully into alignment with the other chakras. Then our chakra system becomes a pure unified bridge of light.

Every soul, from the moment it is created, has within it a small facet of archangel energy. This acts as a magnet and translator, so that every single human has the ability to connect to angels. This attraction operates when we are ready. It is this that enables a third-dimensional being to access angelic help. We are all in tune with the angels at some level.

Archangel Mallory is the Keeper of Ancient Wisdom for this universe. He is a lustrous deep gold, which transforms into rich burgundy when he is actively pursuing a project. In the Golden Era of Atlantis, the high priests and priestesses, inspired by Archangels Christiel and Mallory, took the ninth-dimensional Gold Ray of Christ and formed a pool of energy with it for the use of humanity. The people were able to step down the frequency of the Pool of Christ Light and draw energy from it for love, healing, wisdom and protection and also to create projects with love.

When the causal chakra is open and activated, it is a gateway to the angelic kingdom so that we can communicate with beings of light on the Gold Ray. However, as soon as we reach the glorious upper levels of the fifth dimension we are in constant two-way communication with them, as were the people of the Golden Era of Atlantis.

Clairvoyants can access, through the third eye, the spirits of those who have passed, whatever dimension they are in. However, when we are working with the causal chakra, which is one of the fifth-dimensional transcendent chakras, we can only connect with the spirits of those who are maintaining a fifth-dimensional frequency. High-frequency spirits, masters, unicorns and angels connect with us through this chakra and it is here that we receive downloads of pure light containing information and knowledge.

The causal chakra is connected to the Moon, which has ascended. The wisdom held by the Moon is concentrated through the causal chakra.

The Causal Chakra of the Planet

The causal chakra of the planet is Tibet, which holds the Divine Feminine light. This is where the etheric retreat of the Great White Brotherhood is located. The White Brotherhood and the Great White Brotherhood are the same organization. The name refers to the purity of white light its initiates must attain and radiate.

The Great Pyramid of Tibet was built by the high priest Zeus, who led his tribe there at the fall of Atlantis. It was created with the guidance and assistance of Archangels Metatron and Christiel. Many years ago it was physically destroyed, but it is still active at an etheric level.

If you step into the Great Pyramid of Tibet in your spiritual body, you can enter a fifth-dimensional tunnel of pure light leading to the Great Library of Porthologos in Hollow Earth. By the time you reach the library, the frequency of the tunnel will have stepped up to seventh-dimensional, raising your energy with it. This will enable you to meet the members of the Great White Brotherhood here.

Lord Maitreya is the head of the Great White Brotherhood. Some of the other masters are Lord Voosloo (the highest-frequency high priest ever to incarnate in Atlantis), Jesus, Paul the Venetian, El Morya and Serapis Bey. If you are ready, you can access and receive the pure White Ascension Flame, representing the pinnacle of purity achieved by alignment to Christ consciousness. Serapis Bey will place this over you.

Visiting Archangel Christiel's Retreat

If you wish to visit Archangel Christiel's retreat in meditation, practise the following:

Visualization to Visit Archangel Christiel's Retreat

1. Prepare a space where you can be relaxed and undisturbed. Light a candle if you can.

2. Sit quietly and breathe comfortably with the intention of visiting Archangel Christiel's etheric retreat over Jerusalem.

3. Ground yourself by visualizing roots going from your feet deep into the Earth.

4. Ask Archangel Michael to place his deep blue cloak of protection around you.

5. Imagine yourself standing on a hilltop shimmering with pure moon-white.

6. Make your hands into a chalice and allow Archangel Christiel to pour pure white love into it.

7. Take your hands and place the energy into your causal chakra above your head.

8. Have a sense of the gateway to the angelic kingdom opening.

9. Picture yourself walking through it and being met by pure white angels singing.

10. Open your arms to ninth-dimensional love and experience paradise.

11. When you are ready, return through the gate, leaving it open.

12. Allow Christ Light to flow through you, flooding those around you and spreading round the planet.

13. Thank Archangel Christiel.

Step 27

Archangel Mariel

The Harmonic Convergence in 1987 heralded the start of a 25-year period of purification to prepare the planet for the Cosmic Moment in 2012. The Violet Flame of transmutation had always been available to humanity, though it had not always been available to the masses, but at the Harmonic Convergence Archangel Zadkiel brought it through in such a way that everyone could access it. He then connected it to the soul star chakras of all, even though these chakras were not active in most people. By doing this he was able to accelerate the transmutation of family and ancestral karma so that the ascension process of individuals could flow.

In the past if any of our ancestors passed over with karma unresolved, other members of the family would have undertaken it. Naturally their souls would have agreed to do so before they incarnated, but there has been a massive amount of this unresolved karma and it has particularly burdened certain families. Brave and sometimes foolhardy souls have allowed themselves to be born into such family lines.

Since the Cosmic Moment in 2012, as a result of further karmic dispensations activated by Archangel Zadkiel and his Violet Flame, the situation has changed. This angelic intervention cleared many soul star chakras. Because of this, they are now able to blaze out and express the knowledge, wisdom and experience that the soul has gathered during its journey.

Archangel Mariel and the Soul Star Chakra

The soul star is a magnificent magenta-coloured chakra that radiates our Divine Feminine wisdom. Magenta is a mixture of bright pink and electric blue. The beautiful pink ensures that everything is actioned from the highest and purest intent of the heart, while the electric blue holds the power of manifestation. The task of this chakra is to bring forward our gifts and talents to help us, our family and humanity as a whole. Archangel Mariel is in charge of it. He works closely with Archangel Mary and together they hold the Magenta Flame of Divine Feminine Love. A mass opening of soul star chakras is now occurring.

The soul star chakra is connected to Orion, the cluster of stars that carries the wisdom of the universe. This chakra is such a powerful manifestation tool that its misuse was one of the factors that caused the destruction of Atlantis. Now humanity is once more being entrusted to use it for the highest purpose.

It is also linked to Chiron, the wounded healer, and Vesta, the mother of the home. Because of its prior misuse, these star systems are lovingly beaming in energy to heal the hearts of all of guilt. Then the angels will help us to balance our masculine and feminine aspects so that we can come into true mastery.

Archangel Mariel's twin flame, Archangel Lavender, carries the high priestess aspect of Divine Feminine love. She helps us to understand our gifts and talents and use them wisely. The softness of her lavender light describes her gentle energy. Using this, she often works with us during sleep, when we are willing, to heal our soul star chakra. She even communicates with our ancestors, sharing our wisdom with them and theirs with us and facilitating forgiveness.

There are 33 petals in the soul star chakra and they are all to do with aspects of love and personal responsibility. Archangel Mariel's task is particularly delicate, for it is critical that our soul star is not opened until we are ready to use our gifts and talents with responsibility and the utmost integrity. Our Higher Selves, working in co-operation with Archangel Mariel, are overseeing this to ensure that we only use our power for the highest good.

The soul star is a very powerful chakra. Here are some examples of how it can be used and will be used in the future:

- To bring something into your life, you can create a vision in your third eye. If you then send this out from your third eye, it is like beaming out your picture with a torch. However, if you raise your energy, bring your vision up to your soul star and project it from here into the etheric, it is infinitely more powerful. Your manifestation beam is activating the molecular structure of your vision. That is potent!

- This chakra was used in ancient times to build the pyramids and other sacred buildings. Such an intense picture of the final vision was beamed from this chakra that its energy altered the gravitational mass of the stones. They could then be lifted accurately into place. Specific sound vibrations were used in conjunction with the light from the soul star chakra to achieve this.

- You can bring up energy from other chakras to project it more powerfully for the highest good. An example would be to raise the pink fifth-dimensional light of love from your sacral chakra and project it from the soul star to set families free from their emotional bonds. Or you could raise the vibrant orange fifth-dimensional light from your navel chakra and pour it onto towns or communities to bring the inhabitants into harmony. Certain musical notes can facilitate this.

When we all have full use of our soul star chakra, we will all be totally self-sufficient. In addition, wondrous and magnificent things will be achieved in the world.

The blueprint of Golden Ascended Atlantis, including the spiritual technology of the Atlanteans, their understanding of nature, their capacity to create joyful flow within cities and their ability to access wisdom from the stars, is held within the soul star of all living beings. When we access this with wisdom, it will enable us to create the golden cities of the future.

Archangel Mariel's Retreat

Archangel Mariel's retreat is above the Himalayas. He chose this spot because it has the highest frequency on Earth.

Visualization to Visit the Retreat of Archangel Mariel

1. Prepare a space where you can be relaxed and undisturbed. Light a candle if you can.

2. Sit quietly and breathe comfortably with the intention of visiting Archangel Mariel's retreat.

3. Ground yourself by visualizing roots going from your feet deep into the Earth.

4. Ask Archangel Michael to place his deep blue cloak of protection around you.

5. Picture your soul star chakra above your head, radiating a majestic magenta light. As you focus on it, it becomes electric blue.

6. See Archangel Mariel radiating gloriously above you.

7. He reaches down to touch your soul star and fully activate it.

8. Feel unconditional love flood you, and as you do so, know you are responsible for your planet.

9. Picture within your third eye a place or situation as if it is fully healed.

10. Let this picture now form in your soul star.

11. Beam out this magnificent fifth-dimensional picture from your soul star.

12. Ask Archangel Mariel to energize this picture for the highest good of all.

13. Thank Archangel Mariel.

Step 28

Archangel Metatron's Retreat

Archangel Metatron's retreat is in the etheric above the temple of Luxor in Egypt. It is the hub of the wheel of intergalactic light, surrounded by 12 sub-temples, the temples of the 12 rays. While these are temporary fixtures, Archangel Metatron's etheric temple has existed in the ninth-dimensional overlay since the beginning of the Atlantis experiment 260,000 years ago.

From this temple Archangel Metatron oversees every aspect of the ascension process on Earth. He ensures that everyone is exactly where they need to be and that light is being applied in the correct quantities and in the right place. His temple is a buzzing metropolis of higher-dimensional activity and he is busier now than he has ever been.

We can ask to visit Archangel Metatron's temple to receive his blessing or his ascension cloak, as well as to receive instructions about our ascension path, and guidance about our role in the ascension process and how we may distribute our light.

There are many effective methods of building our personal light on our ascension pathway and Archangel Metatron is the master of this subject. He is pure light and the creator of the illuminated fabric of our very existence. Visiting his retreat in the inner planes is one of the most powerful methods of boosting our spiritual growth.

The 12 Sub-temples

The 12 sub-temples are run by representatives of the Intergalactic Council. These structures were put in place in 2012 at the Cosmic Moment and will remain with our planet until the ascension process is complete in 2032. Each reflects the light of the 12 rays.

Since 2012 the colour frequencies of the rays have changed, in some cases only subtly, but in others, colours within the rays have blended to create a higher energy.

Temple of Ray 1

When you are ready to think constructively and empower yourself to walk your allotted ascension path with open-hearted love, you can ask to visit this temple. The colour is deep radiant purple.

Temple of Ray 2

When you are ready to balance your life so that you live in freedom and truth, you can ask to visit this temple. The colour is a glorious sunshine yellow.

Temple of Ray 3

When you are ready to use your creative potential to serve the planet, you can ask to visit this temple. In this ray spirituality merges with science to bring forward the advanced technology and loving creativity that will enable our planet to ascend gloriously. It brings through the vibration of the crystal technology that powered Golden Atlantis. The colour is a sparkling pink peach.

Temple of Ray 4

When you are ready to bring back the pure white light of the Great White Brotherhood and the Ascension Flame of Golden Atlantis, you can ask to visit this temple. This ray enables you to vibrate with the truth of your heart to connect to the angelic realms. It is the essence of Archangel Gabriel and is pure crystalline white.

Temple of Ray 5

When you are ready to tune in to the secrets of nature so they can be revealed in their purest form (for nature holds the answers to everything on this plane), you can ask to visit this temple. This ray radiates pale orange, crystalline white and the green of nature.

Temple of Ray 6

When you are ready to connect to pure unconditional love, you can ask to visit this temple. You go to this chamber when you truly want the colours of love stroked into your aura. This ray vibrates on very spiritual pink-violet.

Temple of Ray 7

When you are ready to see everything from an angelic perspective, you can ask to visit this temple. Here lower frequencies are transmuted as you look through a cosmic diamond to see a higher spectrum of pure clear white light. You truly know there is nothing to forgive, for all is one and you know all things.

Temple of Ray 8

When you are ready to open up in a blaze of diamond light to experience the joy and peace of universal oneness, you can ask to visit this temple. The stream of light from this ray is gold, diamond and luminous topaz.

Temple of Ray 9

When your soul is so aligned to service with joy that this is your greatest inspiration, you can ask to visit this temple. You enter through a rainbow of light into the orange and gold of Archangel Metatron himself and all that is not love in your aura flows gently away and is replaced with higher love.

Temple of Ray 10

When you are ready for new beginnings on your soul journey, you can ask to visit this temple. As you immerse yourself in the tender leaf-green of this chamber, new golden doors start to open in your life. This strengthens your link to the invisible realms of elementals, angels and unicorns.

Temple of Ray 11

When you open up to the love, healing and wisdom of the Divine Feminine, you can ask to visit this temple. You see everything on the planet in balance and harmony as the translucent aquamarine light flows into you.

Temple of Ray 12

When you receive an invitation to enter this temple, a white-gold diamond is placed over your aura. Each facet clears and sharpens your energy and brightens your light, enabling you to think, act and feel like an ascended master. You are bathed in the higher aspects of the Christ Light.

Visualization for Visiting Archangel Metatron's Retreat

1. Prepare for meditation. Ensure you are relaxed, protected, grounded and undisturbed.
2. Call to the mighty Archangel Metatron and ask to visit his glowing central temple of light.
3. You are standing in front of enormous breathtaking golden gates. You knock, and they swing open. In your head you hear the music of the angelic hosts.
4. Walking through the golden gates, you follow a shifting liquid golden path. This shimmers and lights up in the direction of your travel.
5. You reach a magnificent golden hall, festooned with shining diamonds and liquid light, flowing and dancing before you.

6. Archangel Metatron awaits you. He is like the centre of the brightest Sun you have ever seen, but the brightness is easy on your eyes.

7. He lovingly greets you and asks you to be seated on an amazing golden throne.

8. As you sit down, you feel yourself light up with the power of 1,000 Suns.

9. Archangel Metatron asks you what your personal hopes are for yourself and for the Earth. How do you see yourself serving humanity and Gaia in your ascended role?

10. You tell him your most heartfelt wishes for yourself, humanity and the planet.

11. Lovingly, he takes your wishes in the palm of his hand and magnifies them with his incredible light.

12. He hands this light back to you by placing it in your Stellar Gateway, above the top of your head.

13. You feel your ascension pathway being massively accelerated and light fills every facet of your being. You sit with your eyes closed, absorbing this divine gift.

14. Archangel Metatron places his wings around you and shows you Earth in its ascended aspect. Every person, animal, tree, plant and insect is living in total oneness with their home planet. Love fills the air around them.

15. Thank Archangel Metatron and leave his beautiful retreat.

16. Open your eyes and take your illumination into the ascending world.

Step 29

Archangel Zadkiel

A rchangel Zadkiel is serving this planet by providing the alchemical magic of the Violet Flame in its many facets. He has been offering this service since the dawn of Atlantis, when humans first took physical bodies.

In the very first experiment of Atlantis, the people were provided with everything they needed. It was a cornucopia of delight. However, they did not appreciate all that was given to them without any effort on their part. Lower frequencies and densifications immediately became a challenge, so the Violet Flame was dispensed by the Intergalactic Council as a tool to assist them in transmuting these energies. From this first experiment until the fifth one, when the Golden Era developed, the Violet Flame was one of the most used of the spiritual tools.

Archangel Zadkiel's retreat is in the etheric above Cuba. During the earlier experiments of Atlantis, before the Golden Era, this was the most easterly point of that continent.

Lady Amethyst is the twin flame of Archangel Zadkiel and, as her name suggests, she transmits a very pure and clear yet gentle and soothing healing light. It resonates at a different frequency from that of Archangel Zadkiel but has the same transmuting power.

There are many other shades of light within their repertoire. These run from deep dark violet, which reaches and transmutes the lowest frequencies, to iridescent pale mauve to alchemize situations that need to be purified for the highest good.

Dragons of the Violet Flame

In co-operation with Archangel Gabriel, Archangel Zadkiel created and brought forward a new dragon energy to work in harmony with the dragon forces currently assisting our ascension process. Once the portals of Honolulu and Andorra opened in 2012, the number of dragons and other elementals on this planet increased a millionfold. As part of this inspirational assistance the archangels created dragons of the Violet Flame as living conscious tools to transmute areas of intense density. These are fifth-dimensional elemental dragons.

When an area needs to be cleansed, the fourth-dimensional dragons charge in to burn up the lowest energies. The Violet Flame dragons follow them, transmuting anything that is left and harmonizing the area. Finally Archangels Zadkiel and Gabriel come in and place the Cosmic Diamond Violet Flame in position to hold the energy at the highest frequency for as long as possible.

Violet Flame Clearing of the Earth's Grid

In order to establish a unified Christ consciousness grid on the planet and fortify the ascension process, Archangel Zadkiel's work of transmuting the lower energies is of utmost importance. It is only when the frequency is pure and clear that the grid can be established and solidified at a fifth-dimensional level.

In 2014 there were massive dispensations of the Violet Flame authorized by the Intergalactic Council to accelerate the ascension process. For example, on 7 July 2014 angels of the Violet Flame and Violet Flame dragons were strategically placed in grid formation all round our planet. On the instruction of the Intergalactic Council, Archangels Zadkiel and Gabriel poured in a massive download of the Cosmic Diamond Violet Flame everywhere. The grid of angels and dragons then directed this into specific areas of high need. This was an incredibly powerful process that was felt or perceived by most people at some level as the energy rose by several octaves after this.

While on a surface level this may not have made any ostensible difference to areas of conflict, energetically the consciousness of everyone worldwide was raised. By 2032 the frequency of humanity will no longer support the acting out of egos.

The remarkable grace being offered to humanity by the use of these dispensations helps our ascension process to leap forward. At the same time it is our responsibility to send in the Violet Flame and the Violet Flame dragons into areas of challenge, so that we too are making a difference.

Crystal and Human Reactivation

Crystals programmed with the wisdom of Lemuria and Atlantis that are within the ground or under the ocean are now being reactivated by the raising of the frequency on Earth. Archangel Zadkiel is transmuting any energies that these crystals have absorbed over the last millennia and then illuminating them. This too will dramatically increase the levels of light on the planet and solidify the connection between terrestrial Earth and the seventh-dimensional etheric centre of our planet, Hollow Earth.

The light codes that are pouring out from Helios, the Great Central Sun, are also triggering these crystals. In addition the crystals are activating the DNA within human beings.

Archangel Zadkiel works through the colour violet, so that anyone wearing it or driving a car of that colour or sitting in a room decorated in a shade of mauve will be attuned to his energy. At an unconscious level they have received a prompting from him.

Our woods and forests hold much light, but lower energies are attracted to them and pockets of density hide within them. You can help the entire nature kingdom by invoking the Violet Flame down through a tree into its roots and visualizing it spreading from tree to tree throughout the root network of the planet. Once the flow of the Violet Flame has been established, it will continue, for you have created a Violet Flame portal through that tree.

The same principle applies to all things, including your home. You can really make a difference by drawing the Violet Flame energy down through a prison, a school or a hospital, for example.

Visualization to Meet Archangel Zadkiel

1. Prepare a space where you can be relaxed and undisturbed. Light a candle if you can.

2. Sit quietly and breathe comfortably with the intention of meeting Archangel Zadkiel.

3. Ground yourself by visualizing roots going from your feet deep into the Earth.

4. Ask Archangel Michael to place his deep blue cloak of protection around you.

5. Imagine yourself in a beautiful sparkling amethyst crystal cave.

6. In front of you is a six-pointed star glowing bright violet. Sit at the centre of it.

7. Feel the wondrous Archangel Zadkiel standing beside you, an Illumined Being of the purest light.

8. The violet light fills every cell of your body as Archangel Zadkiel links hands with you.

9. Focus on an area on the planet that needs to be transmuted into a higher light.

10. See the fourth-dimensional dragons clearing the lower energies. Then the Violet Flame dragons swirl through the area, lighting it up with pure violet.

11. Now you and Archangel Zadkiel fly together and place a diamond of pure light and intention to hold the new frequency in place.

12. See the whole place glowing with a fifth-dimensional light.

13. Thank the dragon elementals and Archangel Zadkiel.

Step 30

Archangel Joules

Archangel Joules is in charge of the oceans. His colour is a magnificent deep aquamarine green and his etheric retreat is in the centre of the Bermuda Triangle, where the Great Crystal of Atlantis lies. This forms a seventh-dimensional portal and creates a link between Source and Hollow Earth.

Waters

Water carries the love and wisdom of the universe. Since 2012 it has also been lit up by the golden Christ Light. Waters everywhere are rising in frequency and Archangel Joules oversees the ramifications of this from his retreat.

Because the oceans are great storehouses of the universal light, and the tides and currents spread it, the new frequencies held in water are having a dramatic impact everywhere.

Archangel Joules works in close alignment with Poseidon, the master of water, who was a high priest in the Golden Era of Atlantis. He understood the cosmic qualities of water – how it purifies, blesses and sanctifies people and situations. Through the waters, if you ask, he will link you to the Music of the Spheres to access the sounds of your perfect divine blueprint. Then you can ask him to start to reinstate it in your merkabah.

Together Archangel Joules and Poseidon look after the tectonic plates of the planet. The Earth's surface is made up of a series of large jigsaw pieces that are constantly moving.

At a physical level, friction between these creates mountains, volcanoes, earthquakes and ultimately tsunamis. At a spiritual level, Poseidon and Archangel Joules oversee everything that happens. Lower energies roll from the centre of the plates to the outside edges. Where two plates meet at a point at which negativity has gathered, it must be cleared. This is done by the eruption of a volcano in order that fire can transmute the old into higher frequencies – or an earthquake takes place. Underwater volcanoes and earthquakes can also result in tidal waves carrying love energy that washes away karma on land. The overall plan is vast and it is meticulously planned hundreds of years in advance.

Coral reefs are created on the underwater formations in places where the energy has been transmuted to the fifth dimension. As a result all coral reefs hold fifth-dimensional energy and have a two-way connection with Hollow Earth: the wisdom from Hollow Earth flows through the reefs into the waters and at the same time the reefs transmit information about the oceans to Hollow Earth. All the fish on coral reefs are fifth-dimensional.

Archangel Joules naturally works with the masters and angels of Helios and those of the Moon. Both the Sun and Moon influence the waters of the planet. The golden angels of Helios and the silver lunar angels appear *en masse* at the full Moon and also at times of need to influence the waters and add their qualities of divine masculine and feminine perfection to them. Together they spread nets of gold and silver light imbued with higher love over the planet. These gold and silver nets of love and light dissolve into the waters and profoundly affect the frequency of the oceans and marine life. At certain glorious times of divine dispensation and benevolence, they hold the divine template for divine masculine and feminine balance and unconditional love over the planet so that people can receive illumination for a penetrating instant.

Directed by Archangel Joules and Poseidon, Neptune, the elemental master of water, supervises the undines. They are the elementals who cleanse the oceans and for thousands of years they have co-operated with the fish to purify the waters. Recently, however, with modern-day pollution, this task became too much for them, so little water elementals called kyhils were invited from another universe to visit Earth. In exchange for experiencing our planet and taking this knowledge back to their home planet, they are helping to consume and transmute the current complex chemical contamination. As they do so, they are preparing the waters for their role in the new Golden Age. Mermaids continue to look after the flora and fauna of the oceans.

There are four mighty beings who also co-operate with Archangel Joules to influence the waters and add high-frequency energies to them:

- Archangel Metatron pours the qualities of faith and higher ascension into the waters to help us hold the vision of a fifth-dimensional world.

- Archangel Butyalil holds the blueprint of the cosmic plan and ensures that everything, including the planets, moves in divine harmony. He spreads the information through water, including the water in the cells of our body. This influences us to flow in accordance with the divine plan for our life, bringing forward our innate gifts and qualities so that we can do so. When the sacred geometry of the cosmic plan aligns with that of our personal fifth-dimensional blueprint, huge possibilities open up and we see for a moment our divine magnificence.

- The unicorns transfer their purity, enlightenment and illumination right into the waters.

- Archangel Mary spreads Divine Feminine love and compassion through water and touches us with these qualities when we are ready to accept them.

In addition the oceans and lakes hold the light from other star systems. Like the forests on the surface, the oceans store the wisdom and light from distant universes, ready to release it when the frequency of the planet rises. If we are ready to receive any of these keys and codes, they will automatically be transferred into the cells of our body when we are in water. This is why bathing, swimming and showering offer such huge opportunities for transformation. When we bless water as we swim, bathe, shower or drink, we raise it to a fifth-dimensional frequency. Then these mighty beings can fill the cells of our body with their light.

Aquatic Beings

Archangel Joules also works with all aquatic beings. Fish originate from Pisces and are on a mission to cleanse and clear the waters of the ocean, as well as to help it maintain its frequency. They resonate between the third and fifth dimensions. Tiny fish are part of a group soul on its way to ascension, like every sentient being. Part of the ascension programme of all marine life is fulfilled by bringing in the harmonics of the angels to keep the vibration of the oceans high.

Individualized fish are all fifth-dimensional. For example, dolphins, from Lakumay, the ascended aspect of Sirius, are holding the wisdom and knowledge of Atlantis. They have been waiting for us to be ready to receive it and now, because the frequency everywhere has risen, they are able to transfer it to those humans who are fifth-dimensional.

Whales come from a distant asteroid in the 10th-dimensional universe of Shekinah – incidentally, the same one that hens come from! These mighty beings carry huge amounts of high-frequency light and love, which they share with ocean beings. They do a magnificent job of maintaining the vibration of the oceans.

Sharks, from Nigellay, the ascended aspect of Mars, patrol the oceans. These creatures are martial, but they also carry the qualities of the peaceful warrior.

Turtles, from Jumbay, the ascended aspect of Jupiter, spread the qualities of higher enlightenment and cosmic abundance.

Rays, from the Pleiades, spread healing and joy into the waters.

All these individualized beings are highly evolved creatures. Humans cannot do anything to them without the permission of their souls. They sacrifice themselves deliberately to remind us how important pure clean oceans are.

Connecting with Archangel Joules

You can experience the following exercise as a visualization or you may prefer to lie in a bath, river, lake or ocean and do it!

Visualization to Connect with Archangel Joules

1. Imagine you are floating safe and relaxed in beautiful clear waters.

2. Let golden roots go down from you through the oceans so that you ground yourself into Hollow Earth.

3. You are within the awesome seventh-dimensional portal of Archangel Joules, bathed in beautiful deep aquamarine green light. Feel Archangel Joules connecting with you.

4. Bless the waters with these words or thoughts:

   'I invoke a glorious blessing of love and wisdom on the waters surrounding me. May they be raised to the fifth dimension.'

5. Feel the cells of your body opening like flowers, receptive to the energy you are about to receive from the four mighty beings who work with water.

6. Ask Archangel Metatron to bless the waters and sense his light entering your cells.

7. Call a unicorn and visualize its great horn of spiralling light pouring pure white illumination into the waters.

8. Invoke Archangel Mary and sense her aquamarine light of love and compassion flowing round you.

9. Invite Archangel Butyalil to align you with the cosmic currents. Relax more deeply so that you can see your divine magnificence.

10. Ask Poseidon and Archangel Joules to place your fifth-dimensional etheric blueprint into your energetic body and connect you to the Music of the Spheres.

11. Be aware of the angels singing over you and sense the harmonics flowing over you like liquid light.

12. Relax and ask for your blueprint to be activated.

13. When you are ready, thank the archangels and Poseidon and return to waking consciousness.

Step 31

Archangel Purlimiek, Angel of Nature

The awesome and mighty Archangel Purlimiek holds, with the ninth-dimensional Master Pan, the divine blueprint for our fifth-dimensional natural world. His focus is on Earth, the blue-green planet of this universe, because we have such a unique physical ecosystem. Archangel Purlimiek has worked quietly behind the scenes for thousands of years. Now he is stepping into prominence and is spearheading a co-ordinated plan for the nature kingdoms of Earth.

His etheric retreat, through which he accesses Earth, is Great Zimbabwe in Africa, one of the four two-way inter-dimensional portals of the planet. The other three are Stonehenge, which is a slightly open seventh-dimensional portal; Tibet, the portal of peace; and Machu Picchu, Peru, which is under the jurisdiction of Commander Ashtar.

The Experiment of Physical Form

We are very blessed to live on a planet that enjoys such a cornucopia of nature. It has not always been so. Right up to the end of Lemuria the beings here were etheric and had no physical form. At the cusp of Lemuria and Atlantis the Aborigines incarnated in human bodies in order to ground the energy of the Lemurian age. They were heart-centred, operated from the right brain and brought with them a huge love of the land and understanding of the natural world. They were placed in

Australia so that they were entirely separate from the Atlanteans and various other experiments starting to take place on Earth at the time.

Because these new humans needed to experience the senses, including taste and touch, as well as support a physical body, new and bountiful nature poured from the heart of Source. Glorious trees and plants were seeded. Everything needed to help the new humans was provided. The Aborigines had an inborn understanding of how to use the plants for nourishment, healing, warmth and shelter.

When the experiment of Atlantis was formulated, the curriculum was that all spiritual beings volunteering to participate were to take a body. Like the Aborigines in Australia, the Atlanteans had to feed, water and nurture their physical form. They were vegetarian, eating only plant products. Within the codes of nature everything they could possibly need was provided. Much of the information they required to understand how to use trees and plants was pre-programmed into their consciousness. The high priests and priestesses of Atlantis taught the earliest settlers everything else that they needed to know.

Every aspect of nature was designed by the Great Divine Director to sustain the ongoing experiments on our planet. This mighty being, who serves on the Intergalactic Council and thinks through the divine plan for all the universes, prepared the long-term strategy for Earth. Trees were seeded for food, shelter, medicine, spiritual comfort, oxygen and fire. When they died, their carcasses would bed down into the earth and over centuries become oil to lubricate the tectonic plates and coal for fuel in one possible future. When plants died, they provided the compost to nurture future plants.

In addition, every single tree and plant emitted a quality to help humans and animals. For example, beech trees radiate an energy that helps us forgive others and heal our own traumas. People automatically walk in woodlands when they need solace or to think through a challenge, often without realizing how much the trees are affecting their consciousness.

At first everyone appreciated nature and was grateful for everything. They automatically thanked the divine for the cornucopia of fruit and vegetables that was provided. This was part of the energetic karmic exchange.

The early Atlanteans co-operated with the ethereal elementals to support plants. By talking to the elementals and caring for plants with them, they formed a symbiotic relationship that benefitted the entire planet. They worked with the phases of the Moon and planted at the most propitious time for seeds to grow or crops to be harvested. At that time, all living creatures had a plant diet. Animals only became a source of food when the energies became lower at a later date. In the early days, everything flourished and the plant diet fostered a sense of peace and harmony between all creatures engaged in the experiment.

The Colours of Nature

Archangel Purlimiek vibrates on a beautiful Blue-Green Ray. He carries all the frequencies of the greenery of the original natural world. This colour was chosen to bring everything into balance and keep it there. It radiates the divine vibration of harmony and healing.

As the experiment continued, it was decided to bring in colours, each one vibrating with archangel energy to give the people and animals a wider experience. Where Archangel Uriel's confidence and worth were required, yellow flowers blossomed. To bring in purity and innocence, Archangel Gabriel's white flowers were visible. Pink flowers poured out love.

Until very recent times people valued the perfume of flowers and this was because they were unconsciously breathing in the essence of the archangels. For example, the perfume of a rose brings in the keys and codes of cosmic love from Archangel Mary.

The Harmony of Nature

Archangel Purlimiek and his millions of blue-green angels sing the notes of nature to keep everything in harmony. Unless they have a different agreement, if two plants or trees wish to occupy the same space, one of them will automatically withdraw its energy so that the other can flourish. This harmonic sacrifice has enabled nature to hold its high energy.

Nature brings balance and accord to all sentient beings. It harmonizes the heart, relaxes it and opens the cells of the entire body.

Since 2012 the frequency has risen dramatically and all of nature has become fifth-dimensional. Yes, some plants still have stings or barbs, but these are no longer used actively to defend. They are relics of a time when they were a survival strategy and will eventually withdraw. As their divine nature reinstates itself, plants and trees will try to defend themselves by raising the frequency of their antagonists and surrounding them in peace. In that way, everyone is safe.

You can call on Archangel Purlimiek to help if someone is cutting down a tree unnecessarily. One of his angels will rush to the place to try to raise the consciousness of the person who is doing this. As people everywhere are now raising their frequency, angels frequently succeed in changing people's attitudes.

Trees are sentient beings. If you must cut down a tree or lop a branch, mentally tell the tree first so that it has an opportunity to withdraw its energy.

Elementals

It is Archangel Purlimiek who co-directs the nature spirits, along with Pan, and the beings in charge of the individual elements.

In the forests, for example, elves, little etheric beings of the element earth, look after the trees. They were invited to our planet by Archangels Purlimiek and Butyalil. Fauns, a mixture of elements of earth, air and water, help to balance the energy of forests through photosynthesis. They are rarely seen.

Angels always work for the highest good of all. As nature ascends, many archangels are merging their energies to help it reach its highest potential. Our blue-green planet is becoming one of natural love and harmony.

Nature's Codes

The Great Divine Director ensured that the answers to all questions were encoded into nature. If you walk out in nature with a question in your mind and ask for an answer to come to you, you will see something or have a moment of illumination that brings a new understanding or a solution.

Visualization to Connect with Archangel Purlimiek

1. Prepare a space where you can be relaxed and undisturbed. Light a candle if you can.

2. Sit quietly and breathe comfortably with the intention of connecting with Archangel Purlimiek.

3. Ground yourself by visualizing roots going from your feet deep into the Earth.

4. Ask Archangel Michael to place his deep blue cloak of protection around you.

5. Find yourself in a beautiful glade filled with grass and wild flowers, surrounded by trees.

6. Relax against the trunk of a tree and feel its energy enfolding you.

7. Archangel Purlimiek is floating through the trees, a magnificent blue-green light. His great light is forming round you, so that the codes of nature are merging with your aura.

8. One tree is standing out to you. Tune in to it and sense what it needs. Thank it for being there.

9. Sense or see the colours radiating from the bright green grass and the cascades of multi-coloured flowers.

10. See the natural world from a higher perspective.

11. Thank Archangel Purlimiek and watch him float away.

Step 32

Archangel Fhelyai, Angel of Animals

Archangel Fhelyai is the angel of animals. He has stepped in from another universe to help all creatures on Earth to fulfil their true destiny during this time of opportunity. He is a glorious luminous buttercup yellow, which becomes pure white when he is fully engaged on a mission.

He and his angels watch over animals throughout their lives. When an animal is sick, Archangel Fhelyai's angels comfort and support it. Just like humans, many animals need to be prepared for their death. When that is the case, Fhelyai's angels will be with them, encouraging and helping them for as long as is needed before their passing.

In addition, one of Archangel Fhelyai's angels is present at the birth and death of every single animal. So too is one of Archangel Azriel's angels of birth and death. Archangel Azriel's angels are also with every human for the transitions at both ends of their life. No human or animal goes through either of these initiations alone.

If an animal is being ill-treated, you can offer a prayer to the angel of animals to help it. Archangel Fhelyai will endeavour to impress on someone the desire to rescue the creature. Alternatively, he will try to raise the consciousness of the owner so that they change their behaviour towards it.

Archangel Fhelyai's angels also encourage animals to believe in themselves, for each one has a soul mission for their life just as humans do. For example, pandas are close to the mighty Archangel Mary and co-operate with her to connect people to the Cosmic Heart so that we can open our heart to higher love.

Archangel Fhelyai helps all animals to accelerate their ascension process and experience all that they can. At the Cosmic Moment in 2012, 58 per cent of animals moved into the fifth dimension. By 2014 this had risen to 73 per cent. As a whole, animals are more evolved than humans and are actively teaching us. If you need assistance on your ascension path, an animal may appear to offer you an appropriate experience or lesson.

Incoming Animals

Like humans, animals come from all over the universes to experience life in a physical body on Earth. They incarnate to explore life with the right brain and from the heart. Monkeys, for example, originate from the 10th-dimensional universe of Shekinah and are highly evolved beings. However, they are learning in a completely different way from us, through their right brain and heart.

Because Earth is so closely connected with the four planets, stars and galaxies, the Pleiades, Orion, Sirius and Neptune, that are helping us ascend, many animals are arriving from these places, often with the purpose of helping us on Earth. Usually they are demonstrating by example.

The Pleiades is a star cluster that accesses blue heart healing energy from Source and steps it down to radiate it elsewhere. Pandas, sheep, pigs – and bees, who are fifth-dimensional insects – come from the Pleiades. They all hold this healing light in their energy fields and it flows from them to people, other animals, nature and into the Earth itself.

The 12 Masters of Orion hold the wisdom of the universe. This means that they have the wisdom to use knowledge for the highest good of all. Bears, cats, giraffes, goats, hedgehogs, red squirrels and rabbits come from this constellation and all carry part of the wisdom of the universe in their energy fields. For example, rabbits, who work with Archangel Gabriel, touch people's hearts with love and compassion and help them see situations from a higher perspective, while cats raise the frequency of a home and protect it from lower energies trying to enter.

Sirius is a star and the 12 Masters of Sirius receive spiritual technology and sacred geometry from Source and pass it on to us when we are ready. Cows, horses, deer, camels, elephants and dogs originate from here and help us to access the new. Camels hold a great deal of information in their energy fields and are waiting to transfer it telepathically to us when we are energetically ready. Dogs show their owners such unconditional love, fidelity and devotion that it keeps their hearts open. This enables them to download knowledge more easily.

Neptune is the planet of higher spirituality, holding the wisdom and knowledge of Lemuria and Atlantis. The Masters of Neptune agreed that rats and mice could come to Earth on a special mission to clear physical and etheric rubbish on our planet. When rubbish is cleared, it allows us to open up to our true gifts and potential.

In addition to the animals that incarnate from the ascension planets, guinea pigs come from Venus with the mission of healing the hearts of those who are abused or wounded.

Kangaroos and wallabies enter from Nigellay, the ascended aspect of Mars, bringing in the energy of the peaceful warrior. At the end of Lemuria the Aborigines of Australia incarnated to ground the Lemurian light, and kangaroos and wallabies came in at the same time with the same purpose. Wherever they go, they spread Lemurian healing and the light of the peaceful warrior down the ley lines.

A Portal for Animals at Yellowstone, USA

At the Cosmic Moment in 2012 a vast portal for nature and animals started to open at Yellowstone, USA. It will be fully open by 2032. The energy now pouring from here is yellow, exactly the same shade as the archangel of animals. As this light spreads, it is touching and assisting all animals, wherever they are. It is also influencing our minds and hearts, showing us the cosmic truth that animals are mighty beings in their own right and must be treated with honour and respect in order for the whole planet to ascend.

Archangel Fhelyai's Retreat

Archangel Fhelyai's retreat is on Holy Isle, in the Firth of Clyde, Scotland, UK. He steps his energy down through here to a frequency where he can work with all animals as well as with humans who connect with animals. You can ask to visit his retreat in sleep or meditation to understand and help animals better.

Visualization to Meet Archangel Fhelyai

1. Prepare a space where you can be relaxed and undisturbed. Light a candle if you can.

2. Sit quietly and breathe comfortably with the intention of visiting Archangel Fhelyai's etheric retreat.

3. Ground yourself by visualizing roots going from your feet deep into the Earth.

4. Ask Archangel Michael to place his deep blue cloak of protection around you.

5. Invoke the wondrous Archangel Fhelyai and breathe his glorious sunny buttercup yellow light into your heart.

6. Tune in to an animal and send this luminous yellow colour to it.

7. Sense the animal relaxing and send it a telepathic message.

8. Pause to allow a reply to come to you.

9. Draw the magnificent yellow energy from Yellowstone into your energy fields, then spread it to all the animals in the world.

10. Thank Archangel Fhelyai.

Step 33

Archangel Preminilek and the Insects

Archangel Preminilek is in charge of all the insects on the planet. He comes from another universe and steps his energy down through the mountains in the north of Myanmar, which used to be called Burma. Vibrating on a yellow-green frequency, he co-operates with Archangel Purlimiek, the angel of nature, to co-ordinate the tasks of the insects and protect them on their soul journey.

Insects belong to a group soul of about 1,000 and incarnate on Earth to experience life in all its aspects, just as humans and animals do. They range between the third and fifth dimensions.

Fifth-Dimensional Insects

Fifth-dimensional insects – butterflies and moths, ladybirds, ants and bees – are here to serve as well as to learn.

Butterflies and moths step their frequency down from Orion, the constellation of wisdom, and, like birds, act as messengers for the angels. They carry archangel codes in their energy fields and often appear in order to show us the wonder of life, to keep hope in our hearts and to bring us delight. They may fly into funerals to remind us that death is a new beginning or touch us to bring a blessing from the angels.

Ladybirds, also from Orion, bring us happiness and good fortune. If your heart opens at the sight of a rainbow, you draw in a bountiful energy from the universe, enabling a new door to open. Ladybirds bring the same message. If you smile with pleasure when you see one, your heart opens and you attract something good to you. This is why rainbows and ladybirds are universally loved.

The beautiful ladybirds work with the elementals to help plants. They are not just supporting them physically by eating aphids – they help the fairies and sylphs to clear the energy round plants and they communicate with other insects and persuade them to move elsewhere for the highest good. They spread angelic qualities like love, peace, harmony and co-operation.

Ants step their frequency down from Sirius. They are learning and teaching about sacred geometry and their nests are built on these divine principles. Sacred geometry forms angelic gems in the etheric around their homes. These light formations vibrate at a high frequency and this produces magical harmonics. Because they construct their nests using these sacred codes, ants attract the sonics of the angels, who sing over these edifices.

This is why angelic choirs chant harmonies over ancient cathedrals too. When a place is built according to sacred geometric principles, it brings all who enter it into higher harmony. The vibration also spreads an umbrella of peace over the surrounding countryside.

Bees from the Pleiades also build hives based on sacred geometry. These special creatures offer Pleiadean heart healing wherever they go and their honey contains healing properties. Pixies help to ensure that they pollinate as many flowers as possible. All elementals are attracted to nests and hives that radiate angelic vibrations because the high-frequency energy assists their evolution.

The Spiritual Growth of Insects

The spiritual growth of an insect is identical to that of a person! As soon as a human starts to open their heart and become interested in the welfare of others, they move into the fourth dimension. When insects start to care for beings outside themselves, they become fourth-dimensional. Scorpions care for their young, who live on their mother's backs until they are ready to survive independently. And worms aerate the soil as an act of service. This selflessness has helped these insects to evolve into the fourth dimension. Scorpions and worms originate from Neptune.

Every insect, bird, plant, tree and animal has a divine mission on Earth. In the halcyon days of yore, no one would kill a slug or snail, for they knew they had a perfect role in the maintenance of nature: their assignment was to eat rotting plant material and pass it through their systems so that it became manure for future growth. Equally, no slug or snail would dream of eating newly planted lettuces. Furthermore, when elementals and humans worked symbiotically, the elementals would dissuade any insect who manifested an inclination to eat something that was not for them.

Third-dimensional insects such as centipedes, beetles, cockroaches, fleas, flies, ticks and mosquitoes originate from Neptune and each has a role to play on Earth. Centipedes are learning about co-ordination and they teach the skill of harmonious co-ordination by demonstrating it!

Many insects incarnate to serve the planet by breaking down unwanted materials so that they can be recycled for a higher purpose. Beetles do precisely this. Cockroaches have a special mission to go into the darkest and dirtiest places, where they break down the foul waste and faeces to keep nutrients moving around the ecosystem. They do this for creatures such as bats as well as humans. At the same time they clear the low psychic energy that hangs round with this waste.

Because the amount of psychic and physical rubbish on the planet is increasing, Archangel Metatron has invited elementals to come here from another universe. In exchange for accelerated evolution, esaks have come to help clear up after us. These brave elementals work with the insects.

As Atlantis devolved, people needed to be reminded about hygiene, cleanliness and keeping energies clear and moving.

Fleas arrived to offer this reminder. Mosquitoes appeared to prompt people to keep water clean, pure and flowing. Ticks, which are blood-sucking arachnids, teach us that we live in an interdependent world. They are especially drawn to the blood of deer, who are carrying the lessons of trust.

Spiders are universally feared and disliked because they originate in a third-dimensional universe without gravity and have a vibration that is alien to us. They step down through Sirius, where they learn about sacred geometry in the training establishments of that star. They then incarnate to learn from Earth and take this knowledge back to their home universe. They also teach us about the sacred geometry that they use in their webs and about focused patience. Because they come from a universe without gravity, they do not understand or give credence to the limitations of that force. They spin their webs against gravitational pull by holding the vision of the outcome they intend and they succeed. They are teaching us to hold a vision, however impossible it seems, and to overcome the limitations of collective conscious beliefs. This is quite a message for a tiny insect, but they teach it by demonstrating it in their lives.

Crickets and grasshoppers come from Sirius. Their humming and chirruping are not only about mating: the sound vibration calls the elementals and thanks them. Wasps, also from Sirius, build their nests according to sacred geometry and are teaching us the benefits of it. In addition they incarnate to learn and teach about sacrificing yourself for the greater good of the community.

Connecting with Insects

Insects are on a very different frequency band from humans, so it is more difficult for us to tune in to their wavelength than that of other creatures. It is easier to communicate with those insects that are more evolved.

Here is a visualization to visit the angel of insects.

Visualization to Visit Archangel Preminilek, Angel of Insects

1. Prepare a space where you can be relaxed and undisturbed. Light a candle if you can.

2. Sit quietly and breathe comfortably with the intention of visiting Archangel Preminilek's etheric retreat.

3. Ground yourself by visualizing roots going from your feet deep into the Earth.

4. Ask Archangel Michael to place his deep blue cloak of protection around you.

5. Find yourself sitting in a wild, unspoiled place out in nature, where the music is the song of insects.

6. A glorious yellow-green light is approaching and as it reaches you, you find yourself rising up in it as if you are being taken up in a lift.

7. You find yourself in an etheric place, exactly like the wild place where you started.

8. You are surrounded by insects, only some of which you recognize. They are curious but harmless. None of them touches you.

9. You see that there are elementals with them, lovingly helping them.

10. You may want to talk to the energy of a group soul or to a fifth-dimensional insect. You can ask why they came to Earth, what they are learning, how they feel on Earth, what they feel about humans, what it is like in their home star or planet or any other question that feels relevant.

11. When an insect steps forward, notice the sacred geometric structure of its energy field. It may wish to touch your aura with this.

12. And now the gentle yellow-green light is beside you and Archangel Preminilek is looking at you with a benevolent, compassionate smile. 'Insects are the building structures of your world,' he says. 'You cannot exist without them. Treat them as you would like to be treated.'

13. He holds his hand out to you and his great light surrounds you.

14. Thank Archangel Preminilek and find yourself back where you started.

Step 34

Archangel Bhokpi, Angel of Birds

When the curriculum for Atlantis was written, everyone could see and connect with their angels. Birds had nothing to learn, so they were sent to Earth to act as messengers for the angels. Birds vibrate between the third and fifth dimensions. Those that were third-dimensional arrived from Sirius. Those that were fifth-dimensional came from its ascended aspect, Lakumay. In Atlantis they would deliver personal messages or sing in the cosmic news for the day. The vibration of Atlantis rose and fell many times and by the end of the Atlantean era, people were no longer in close contact with their angels, so the program was rewritten and birds took on a more important role. Each species carried specific information in its aura which it imparted to humans either through its song or through its actions.

Archangel Bhokpi is in charge of the bird kingdom. He works with Archangel Metatron to ensure that the songbirds literally tweet in the spiritual news at dawn each day. The dawn chorus was once a very significant way of imparting information about the universal flow, the weather and any special energies that were coming in. Now we can no longer consciously understand it. However, many animals can still do so and have prior warning of weather changes or challenges to come.

Small birds belong to a group soul of about 100. Little songbirds and many waterbirds still belong to this category.

When the group soul ascends to Lakumay, the birds individualize. Some of the ascended birds who have mastered an aspect of life are:

- The albatross, which teaches oneness as it floats in its element with serenity and peace.

- Eagles and condors, who have mastered the element of air.

- Owls, who hold wisdom and teach the elementals in their local areas. They hold the vision of a fifth-dimensional world and try to help people see what needs to be done.

- The parrot family, who have mastered the art of listening so that they can mimic words and sounds.

- Penguins, who demonstrate a perfect balance of yin and yang, feminine and masculine. They connect to Hollow Earth through Archangel Sandalphon and the Earth Star chakra.

- Puffins, who connect to Hollow Earth through Archangel Joules and water so that they express the Divine Feminine.

- Swans, who demonstrate purity and majestic grace.

The Legacy of the Past

The Golden Age of Lemuria left two very important legacies for humanity. One was a deep love of the entire natural world. Hummingbirds, who have ascended, still sing to us of this wonderful energy and to remind us how important the nature kingdom is. If one of these birds comes to our attention, it is reminding us to connect joyously with nature.

The second legacy was the ability of groups to co-operate for the highest good without a designated leader. Migratory birds, such as swallows, swifts, martins and many varieties of goose, demonstrate this. We can watch them fly overhead in harmonious formation, one bird ahead of the others. Seamlessly, another bird will take the lead role for a time, and then another.

This is the way assemblies of ascended humans will run their affairs in the Golden Age to come. Holding, without ego, a desire to serve for the highest good, people will gather and connect telepathically. At any given time one will step forward to activate the communal vision. Decisions will be easily and collectively taken at a higher level, ensuring the comfortable flow of society.

When migratory birds fly above the land, they send healing to nature. They automatically link into the ley lines, lighting them up and raising their frequency. Since 2012 these healing birds have raised their frequency and are now sending light and healing into the new crystalline grid to help power it up and bring it online more quickly. This service work will help the birds ascend to Lakumay.

The Golden Age prior to Lemuria was Mu. Although the beings who lived then were etheric and never took physical form, they did love the Earth and the four stellar connections that are helping our ascension – Neptune, Orion, Sirius and the Pleiades. Today there are representatives of all the Golden Ages living etherically within Hollow Earth. Here beings from Mu are entrusted to keep the wisdom of these four ascension planets, stars and constellations. They also hold a blue flame of love and healing at the heart of each of them.

The beings of Mu understood that mountains are alive and, like all living beings, emit their own notes. The song of most mountains is like angels singing and each one has its own tune. If the mountain is seamed with high-frequency gems and minerals, the notes will be higher and purer. A few mountains are now out of tune and it is time to bring all these sacred places into a new, higher, harmony.

Mu was the time of the dinosaurs. The dinosaur-like pelicans hold the collective memories and wisdom of that time.

Communication with Birds

Angels leave little white feathers as a sign to say they are near or to offer us hope. They can manifest a feather, but this takes energy, so very often a bird will drop one for them to waft into the right place. Angels and birds work together in many ways.

Birds draw our attention to things that we might otherwise have missed. For example, we may turn to look at one that has landed near us and as we do so notice a beautiful flower. A bird may call from the sky and we look up to see an angelic cloud formation.

Visualization to Connect with the Bird Kingdom

1. Prepare a space where you can be relaxed and undisturbed. Light a candle if you can.

2. Sit quietly and breathe comfortably with the intention of connecting with the birds.

3. Ground yourself by visualizing roots going from your feet deep into the Earth.

4. Ask Archangel Michael to place his deep blue cloak of protection around you.

5. Invoke the illumined Archangel Bhokpi and relax as you feel his deep green glow surrounding you.

6. Visualize yourself by the deep blue sea, on a snow-capped mountain or somewhere else in nature.

7. A bird is flying towards you and landing near you. You feel it sending you pure unconditional love.

8. As you tune in to it, you sense you are growing into the body of that bird.

9. Your beautiful feathers are growing. Notice how they feel.

10. Be aware of your eyes – how sharp and clear they are.

11. Gently spread your wings and find you can rise up in your inner world and fly.

12. Experience the exhilaration, the joy, higher vision and wisdom of the bird.

13. Understand how it feels to be a bird, free to flitter or soar or glide.

14. Thank the bird and settle back into your physical body.

15. With Archangel Bhokpi's beautiful light surrounding you, all the birds feel safe with you. Many are approaching you.

16. Take time to listen to them with new understanding and you may receive their messages.

17. Thank the birds and Archangel Bhokpi.

18. When you are ready, return to the place where you started.

Step 35

Archangel Butyalil

Archangel Butyalil is a mighty angel who operates throughout the universes. He is working with Archangel Metatron to co-ordinate the ascending flow of all 12 universes. At present much of his focus is on Earth because of the double-dimensional shift we are undergoing in a 20-year period. We have to rise from the third to the fifth dimension before 2032. This is unheard of in the entire history of the universe.

Two factors caused us to descend into the third dimension. The first was the daring experiment by the Intergalactic Council to allow us free will. The second was the fact that Earth is the solar plexus of the universe and is therefore taking in and transmuting the fear held in this universe. The entire cosmos is now helping us to climb the spiritual mountain as quickly as possible.

Archangel Butyalil is pure white and his etheric retreat is at the meeting point of the four ascension planets above the Earth. Due to the ineffable purity of his light he is only just starting to work with individuals.

One of his tasks is to show us our magnificence, not just as a soul but as an intergalactic being. He has only been able to do this since 2012, as the reflection he shows us of our true self is so brilliant that it would dissolve the Veil of Amnesia that was put in place during the third-dimensional experiment on Earth. This Veil, with seven layers, was put into position for every soul incarnating, so that they would be able to explore the third-dimensional world without realizing who they really were.

Each layer is removed only when our heart is open and we have passed an initiation to test that we are ready. However, sometimes a Veil is partially removed and the final removal takes place at a later date. The unicorns, under the direction of Archangel Butyalil, help to remove these Veils. Archangel Butyalil authorizes every single Veil removal that occurs on Earth, whether it is for a human or an animal.

The Seven Veils

The seven Veils of Illusion or amnesia are:

The Seventh Veil

This red Veil is the furthest from our third eye and is the first to dissolve. The process starts when our soul wakes up and we recognize that we are responsible for everything in our life. As we take mastery of our life and stand in our power, this etheric Veil is automatically removed by our angel under the supervision of our unicorn.

Now our spiritual journey has truly started. We see our existence from a higher perspective. We know we have choices and the responsibility to transform anything we wish.

The Sixth Veil

The first step in the removal of this yellow Veil is when we start to recognize the spirit world and realize that there are other worlds and vibratory beings interwoven with this one. It dissolves fully when we believe in and trust the spiritual beings, from elementals to angels and beyond, to assist us. This requires interaction and our initiation is passed when we have truly handed ourselves over to the higher realms, so that we can help each other.

The Fifth Veil

This is the pink Veil of love. This is the emotional ascension Veil and is one of the most difficult initiations to undertake, as it requires complete detachment of ego. This is the initiation where we lose everything dear to us and have to surrender our heart.

When we have the opportunity to forgive other souls and do so, we hold unconditional love in our heart centre for everyone. We realize that we are all one. At this point we automatically bless the soul involved in hurting us, as well as the situation and the outcome, so that it is all taken to a higher level.

The Fourth Veil

This blue Veil starts to dissolve when we really understand who animals are and that they are on their own soul journey and have their own individual missions for their lives. At the same time we open up to and love nature and the elemental kingdom. When we start to work with animals, nature and the elementals on a psychic and physical level, we transcend duality and separation.

We can help the enlightenment and ascension process on Earth by talking telepathically or during our sleep to those people who need to have a higher understanding of the roles that animals, nature and the elementals play in the great spiritual scheme of life.

The Third Veil

This deep blue Veil is dissolved when we co-operate with the angels and ascended masters for the highest good of the planet. We are now operating from a point of mastery and have become a master. We are using our power to create a higher state of being in everything that we touch and see. We live in true oneness.

The Second Veil

When this violet Veil is removed, we literally see the cosmos from the point of oneness. We know that everything is connected – stars, the trees, the animals, the very fabric of the planet. We achieve universal consciousness and are fully enlightened.

The First Veil

Before 2012 this crystal-clear Veil was only removed once we had passed over, and only then if we were ready. It is now dissolved steadily over the course of our ascension process. Strips are removed by Archangel Butyalil as he gently opens us to the full glory of our cosmic master self.

Connecting with Archangel Butyalil

Archangel Butyalil spreads his energy through water, which permeates the universe and carries the energy of love. To make our connection with him stronger, we can call him in to touch us when we are in a bath, shower, pool or the ocean. This will charge the cells of our body with his energy.

He co-ordinates with the Great Divine Director, the master of the First Ray of the Intergalactic Council, to write the curriculum for those who are ready to train in Seraphina's cosmic school in the inner planes.

It is Archangel Butyalil who takes individuals to Seraphina's retreat where they can start their cosmic work and aspire to become intergalactic ambassadors.

Archangel Butyalil works with Archangel Metatron to ensure that the flow of our ascension plan is running according to divine will. However, his main purpose is to oversee the cosmic flow. He checks that all planets and stars are ascending in harmony together.

If you tune in to Archangel Butyalil's energy in meditation and request it, you will be shown your magnificent piece in the cosmic puzzle. It is then that you will truly realize the magnitude of your soul and how important your presence on Earth is. Your role may appear to be humble, but Archangel Butyalil will show you how important you are to the plan on Earth. Look in the mirror.

Visualization to Look into Archangel Butyalil's Cosmic Mirror

1. Find a place where you can be quiet and undisturbed.

2. Imagine you are standing under a waterfall of shimmering white water.

3. Invoke Archangel Butyalil to touch you at a cellular level with his pure white light, so that every cell of your body is illuminated and you feel him merging with you.

4. He is holding up a vast cosmic mirror in front of you.

5. You see yourself reflected in the glass.

6. Gradually you expand and light up until you can see the vastness of your expanded self, reaching right out to the stars.

7. You can see filaments of your energy reaching through space to distant solar systems, connecting with the essence of your soul.

8. Your light is the universe, transcending space and time.

9. Your breath matches the pulse of the cosmos, illuminating you in harmony with all aspects of your being.

10. Bring this energy into your heart centre.

11. Breathe this energy out to others on their ascension pathway.

12. Thank Archangel Butyalil for this gift and open your eyes.

Step 36

Archangel Azriel

Archangel Azriel is unique in the angelic kingdom for his light is within, which is why he appears black. In fact he offers a glorious golden-white cocoon of angelic safety to every spirit who travels with him.

He is a Power, an angel of the 10th-dimensional frequency, known as the angel of birth and death. One of his angels is present at the birth and death of every single animal and human.

Birth and death are the two biggest initiations that every creature who incarnates undertakes. An initiation takes us, usually through pain, into a higher frequency. Divorce, a house move, examinations and other stressful times are often initiations, and Archangel Azriel, with his twin flame, Archangel Zarah, supports us through these challenges. Archangel Zarah carries Divine Feminine qualities of love, caring and compassion and she tends the needs of those who are in transition. She comforts those who are grieving. These archangels are present at every major initiation in our life. We can ask them to help us with any transitions or initiations we are going through and we will hold ourselves in their cocoon or womb until we feel safe enough to face it and courageously transcend lower limitations to reach a higher frequency.

Birth

In ancient superstitions, crows, rooks and ravens were said to bring bad luck or a warning of danger. Like most superstitions, this was based on a misinterpretation of spiritual truths. These birds work with Archangel Azriel and one is sent to every animal who is about to give birth to warn them to prepare for it. Archangel Azriel also sends one of his birds to remind people to change their attitude or to raise their consciousness or there will be a karmic consequence. No wonder people saw one of his birds just before they suffered misfortune and thought the bird brought them the bad luck. If only they had listened to the message, they could have raised their frequency and averted it. The same applies nowadays, though most people have become unaware that birds are sent as messengers.

When a vulnerable baby is about to be born, the magnificent and tender Archangels Azriel and Zarah bring the new soul into the Earth plane within the safety of the spiritual womb they provide. This helps to cushion the transition moment.

A baby can only be stillborn if it is a soul decision to experience the journey and maybe the landing, but not the trip on Earth. The mother and often the father have made a huge sacrifice in order to allow that soul to have this chance. Being attached to the mother allows the soul to connect with Earth and the moment of entry to our physical world offers them a huge opportunity, even if they do not stay. Archangels Azriel and Zarah will often wait with the spirit of the baby until it is ready to return to the inner planes.

Death

Many people have a sense of heightened awareness when they are near death or are with someone who is dying. They may see or sense dark shadows and be afraid. But Archangel Azriel's glorious angels are showing their dark outer cocoon and only the person in transition sees the light within.

Whether animal or human, Archangel Azriel comes to collect every single soul when they die. Archangel Fhelyai, wonderful yellow angel of animals, is also present at the death of every animal, as well as at its birth.

Archangel Azriel opens his cocoon and most souls gladly step into his blazing, welcoming light to be transported safely home. Often they are accompanied by many other angels and archangels, singing in jubilation. If they ascend into a much higher dimension, many magnificent archangels travel with them in joy and celebration.

Occasionally, however, a human or animal at death may not step into Archangel Azriel's welcoming light. They may be in shock, lost, attached to their children or even tied to alcohol or drugs or worldly goods. In this case an elemental, a wuryl, will be assigned to accompany them at all times until they are ready to go to the heavenly light. Like all elementals, wuryls have raised their frequency since 2012 and this will make it easier for stuck souls to find the light.

If someone dies in a fire or because of fire, Archangel Gabriel will also meet them to heal and help them; if they drown, the great being Poseidon will meet them; if they are buried in an earthquake or avalanche, Lady Gaia herself will be there; and if they pass due to a form of air, such as a hurricane, a unicorn will be present.

Timing

As a mighty Power, Archangel Azriel keeps the Akashic records for every creature in this universe, so he records when a safe birth, death or transition of any sort has been accomplished. He also oversees the co-ordination of every birth and death, ensuring that a soul is in the right place at the right time. What may seem to be right timing for us is not necessarily so for the archangel.

Archangel Azriel works with Archangel Butyalil, who is in charge of the cosmic currents, to ensure that babies are born at the moment when they can catch the tide that will take them into the life they have chosen. Similarly, a person may linger long after people expect them to die or they may die suddenly and inexplicably early. This is so that they can enter the cosmic flow that will propel them to the next experience they have chosen. Some souls wait years for the right cosmic moment for either birth or death. Archangel Azriel co-ordinates matters with other Universal Angels who work throughout the universes to ensure that a soul is in the right universe to experience its next divinely guided step.

Connecting with Archangel Azriel

Archangel Azriel's etheric retreat is very small and is over the mountains of Wales, UK. Because he is working tirelessly throughout the universes, he is rarely there. When you need him during initiations, at birth or on your passing, he is automatically with you, so you don't need to visit his etheric retreat. However, it is appropriate to send him a prayer.

 A Prayer to Archangel Azriel ❖

Beloved Archangel Azriel,

I offer a prayer for all souls who are being born. Please ease their birth and help their mothers during childbirth. Open the hearts of the entire family. Strengthen the bonds of all so that they can support the newly born baby.

I ask you to steady and prepare all souls for the initiations and major transitions they have chosen to undertake in this life.

Be with all those who are dying. Let them see your glorious light so that they feel safe and comforted as you take them home.

Comfort all those who are grieving.

I ask this under grace. So be it.

❖

Step 37

The Seraphim Seraphina

The Seraphim are 12th-dimensional angels who surround the Godhead and sing in the divine vision for Source. There are 144 of these ineffable beings and it has only been in the last few years that a few of them have contacted and worked with humans. Seraphina is one of these. Like all Seraphim, she sings the notes that form the geometric structure of our highest potential.

In her glorious grace Seraphina helps us to strengthen our connection with our Monad and Source. She pours her high-frequency light and tones down to us through the golden ascension thread that always links us to Source. Her assistance expands and strengthens this into a wide and strong bridge, our Antakarana bridge, and ensures it is properly functional all the way to our Monad. She then helps to anchor it by singing it into position. Once our Antakarana bridge is in place, our communication with our Monad becomes pure and clear. Then we receive instructions and guidance for our ascension path directly from our Monad, our own 12th-dimensional aspect.

Seraphina also helps to anchor the fifth-dimensional merkabah round people who have a light percentage of 80 per cent or above by pouring a breath of sound around them. Not only does this apply to individuals, but she can construct worlds using this method. This is the pure power of the Creator.

When you are very clear about what you want to create and your intention is for the highest good, you can tune in to

Seraphina or look at one of her Orbs and focus on your vision. It adds even more power if you chant the Aum or Om, which is the sound of creation. This will draw to you her assistance in becoming a master creator.

Seraphina's School

Seraphina is like a multi-coloured rainbow with many roles. She oversees a vast intergalactic training school for those who have the capacity and desire to serve the cosmos. Hundreds of thousands of humans are serving on this intergalactic level without realizing it. You must have your 12 chakras open and active to do so. You will then visit the training schools while you are asleep to receive instruction from the beings of light who work with Seraphina and certain of the ascended masters. These include Dwjhal Kuhl, Lord Voosloo and Archangel Metatron.

When you aspire to enter Seraphina's training school, she will sing a geometric high-frequency curriculum into your energy fields so that you are attuned to your future service. As you progress, she and her team will continue to oversee every step of your learning pathway.

You may eventually become an inner planes teacher as well as an intergalactic ambassador. Your soul self may be learning about or working in the planetary field while your monadic self is undertaking huge roles in star system management. This includes working for the solar system, including the vibrational management of stars within that field or even inter-universal work. For example, if a planet such as Earth is accelerating into the fifth dimension, the third-dimensional geometric structures round the planet have to be dissolved so that higher-frequency ones can be installed. At present there is a situation here on Earth that has never been experienced before: the third-dimensional Earth structure is being retained as a school for those who wish to continue learning at that level, while a new fifth-dimensional school has already been created in the higher crystalline matrix. The illuminating energies of people who are fully fifth-dimensional are rapidly raising the frequency of everyone else and this will be completed by 2032, when the whole planet with be gloriously fifth-dimensional. Seraphina's rainbow light is holding the fifth-dimensional crystalline school for the time being.

Seraphina's Guidance

Some of the new crystalline children are being guided by Seraphina. She is stepping down her frequency to connect with these children and then raising them up very quickly. This is not necessarily an easy process for the parents to cope with, as they are required to keep their frequency fifth-dimensional. However, at a soul level the parents have chosen this service, which will accelerate their own path.

When groups of people of the right frequency gather together, Seraphina sings over them in a way that is very similar to that in her galactic schools and information is imparted into their energy fields by high crystalline tones. These hold a geometric light shape that contains codes and information that will trigger their own latent knowledge. The notes that Seraphina is bringing to us now are rapidly accelerating the ascension of both individuals and the planet, and are becoming higher by the month.

The auras of trees, animals, insects, elementals, the waters and the land itself are also open to receive Seraphina's diamond crystalline offerings of light. There is a constant process of upgrading taking place. This can be tiring or even overwhelming for all sentient beings. Rest and adjustments to our lifestyle are essential.

Trees, plants and fauna are preparing to take on new forms in harmony with the fifth-dimensional frequencies they have recently attained. For example, they are changing their communication with each other by adjusting the genetic codes within their pollen.

In the Golden Era of Atlantis, trees and plants did not have spikes or thorns. They did not need them, for everyone was harmless. Currently they are having to contend with third-dimensional frequencies within their fifth-dimensional world. They can be greatly assisted if you offer them acknowledgement and gratitude, for this will help them to make their transition graciously.

Connecting Seraphina

As you prepare for this meditation, remember you are undertaking high-frequency work, so ensure that your system is pure and clear. Drink plenty of water.

Visualization to Visit Seraphina in the Inner Planes

1. Sit quietly in your favourite meditation spot. Ground yourself and invoke Archangel Michael's protection.

2. Invoke the mighty Seraphina.

3. You will notice your perception change as the Seraphim energy instantly connects with yours. It feels like etheric honey.

4. You are standing in the grounds of an incredible school or university campus. Pathways to radiant golden buildings are laid out before you. They lead in all directions, changing colours before your eyes.

5. Seraphina stands at the edge of the pathway closest to you, a beautiful being radiating the most incredible love and light. In her hands, she holds a book filled with your soul achievements and those to which you still aspire.

6. You move to stand next to her and you both start to walk towards a stunning construction made of shifting golden light. As you are walking, she tells you that this is the start of your training as a galactic master.

7. You enter the golden building together and you see the universe laid out before you. Planets form and stars are born before your eyes.

8. Seraphina holds a new star in her hands, glowing with cosmic divinity. She hands it to you. You close your eyes and accept this incredible gift.

9. Seraphina stands in front of you and starts to sing, but not in a conventional voice. You feel every molecule of your being rise in frequency as her tone alters your very being.

10. In each cell of your body there is now a set of codes and instructions. Seraphina places her hand gently upon your crown and activates these codes with a single pulse of light.

11. You thank Seraphina and start to leave the cosmic building with her. She tells you that everything that you will ever need will be given to you as you sleep at night. Her blessing is one of the highest gifts in the universe.

12. Your perception changes as you return to your meditation spot and breathe deeply.

13. Open your eyes and smile. You are on the path of a galactic master.

Step 38

The Atlantean Blue Star
Seal Meditation

Energies are rapidly changing at present, with the result that many of the protection methods people have been using are breaking down. The Atlantean Blue Star Seal meditation is a protection meditation either for personal use or to protect space such as a home, school or car. It can be used anywhere and by anyone, but for it to be effective we must trust that once we have invoked it, it will clear our personal space and will protect and support us unconditionally.

We can also apply this energy to other people and places. However, this is only appropriate when applied under the Law of Grace and a request is sent to the Higher Self of the person involved.

This meditation is very powerful and uses the assistance of the fire dragons, who are fourth-dimensional energy clearance experts. Once we invoke them they will burn and transmute any lower vibrations and frequencies to which we direct them. They are especially good at scorching out really stuck, dense energy and are very happy to do so.

The Atlantean technology we are using is called the Blue Star Seal. It is supplied by Thoth and was used by him personally on a daily basis to guard his space and energy during his incarnations in Atlantis and Egypt. It was activated via his soul star chakra and surrounded him in a field of protection that was anchored in the ninth dimension by Archangel Metatron. This would move with him wherever he went as a personal force-field, using the sacred geometric shape of the six-pointed star of Atlantis.

With the help of Thoth and the Blue Ray of Archangel Michael, this protection is now available to us in its primary geometric shape. Any positive energies of our choice can be placed for our benefit within the space of this protective seal. This may be within our aura or energy fields, or in a house or office or somewhere else. Archangel Metatron will then, upon request, hold the Blue Star Seal in our aura until we ask him to release it.

Finally, Archangel Sandalphon will ground us into Hollow Earth via our Earth Star chakra to ensure full stability energetically and to ensure that we do not receive too much energy without an etheric 'lightning rod'. It is up to us how much or how little we place within our aura.

This meditation is only available once our 12 chakras are open and activated. It gives us the opportunity to start working more deeply with these chakras and an idea of their potential and power once fully operational. The more we focus on them and use them, the more effective they will become.

We can also use the meditation to lock our requested frequencies in our fields and hold them there undisturbed. When we use it, Thoth will activate and empower our personal soul star chakra to encourage our ascension.

The meditation is relatively short and easy to apply.

Invocation to Receive the Blue Star Seal

Initial Invocation

1. Say:

    'Beloved Fire Dragons, I, [name], invoke you to clear completely all lower frequencies from my aura, my bodies and fields. I specifically ask you to clear all [for example, fatigue, anxiety, worry, poverty consciousness,

negative etheric energy, negative forces or anything that you know is affecting your energy, space and light].'

Be specific. The fire dragons will clear anything that you want.

2. Sit quietly and visualize them burning away all your 'stuff' with their roaring flames.

3. When you feel clear and calm, ask them to stop.

4. Thank them.

Second Invocation

1. Say:

   'Mighty Thoth, I now invoke the activation of your Blue Star Seal.'

2. Above your head, in the area of your soul star chakra, a bright blue light will activate.

3. Visualize a circular dome of blue light coming down and surrounding you.

4. You are standing in the centre of a bright blue six-pointed star and the dome is surrounding this. This is the geometry of your protection.

5. Call upon the immense and powerful Archangel Michael and ask him to place within your seal any energies of your choice. Here are some examples of beautiful and powerful energies that are perfect to use: the Gold Ray of Christ; the Cosmic Diamond Violet Flame; your monadic connection; Archangel Metatron's ascension energy; the light of your favourite archangels or ascended masters such as the Diamond White Ray of Archangel Gabriel; the Emerald Ray of Archangel Raphael; the soft Pink Ray of love from Quan Yin; Lord Kumeka's Turquoise Ray of deep transmutation. They will give you whatever you want, upon request.

6. Request the amplification of any other positive thing that you require, such as prosperity consciousness; divine, radiant and perfect health; happiness, vitality, confidence or other beautiful qualities. Be sure to ask in positive terms!

7. Ask Thoth and Archangel Michael to amplify and support the Seal.

8. Thank them both.

Final Invocation

1. Say:

> *'Archangel Metatron,*
>
> *I now invoke you to link my Blue Star Seal to your ninth-dimensional frequency.*
>
> *I ask that you now descend a pillar of light down through my Monad, each of my chakras and into Hollow Earth, to be grounded and held by Archangel Sandalphon.*
>
> *Please ensure that a clear and a continual energy flow is established and held until I request you to release this.*
>
> *Thank you.'*

2. Once you have asked him to do this, Archangel Metatron will send a beam of high-frequency light from his ninth-dimensional aspect down through your monadic presence. It will then travel through your Stellar Gateway, causal, soul star, crown, third eye, throat, heart, solar plexus, navel, sacral, base and finally Earth Star chakra and into Hollow Earth.

3. Archangel Sandalphon will then ground this.

Each of your chakras is now fully open and vibrating at a fifth-dimensional frequency.

You are blessed, and fully protected at all times.

Step 39

Karmic Dispensation

At the end of Lemuria a small and select group of souls petitioned Source to be able to experience life in a solid form. When their petition was granted, these became the original participants in the first experiment of Atlantis. With a physical body they were given free will and went through the Veils of Amnesia so they forgot their divine selves and many soon found it difficult to connect to Source.

Their experiences formed the basis for the current human root race. Those observing from the higher realms realized that the experience of life on Earth created a cause-and-effect process that needed a spiritual Law of Karma to make it work. So, from the moment we descended into the third dimension, where we experience polarity, we were subject to the Law of Karma. It was devised so that we could experience what we had done to others. It is the basic learning tool available for the school of Earth. All thoughts, words and actions draw a return of identical energy. Good, warm, loving thoughts, words and deeds are repaid in kind. Positive attracts positive. Negative attracts negative.

During the era of Atlantis, everyone on Earth experienced as much as possible while exploring life at varying frequencies. Whilst this was occurring, however, karma was being generated by every living soul that set foot here, including the great masters. It is very easy to create karma. Every thought, word or deed that we take is measured by this exact law.

We have now reached a point where we are all ready to step off of the wheel of karma and ascend gloriously into the fifth dimension. In order to do this, we need to have cleared the karma accumulated over the course of our lifetimes and quickly learned the lessons involved. It is not just personal karma that needs to be cleared. Many families carry ancestral karma that has built up through generations. Country karma also exists for entire nations.

The Karmic Board

The Board of Karma governs and oversees the application of karma for everyone in the world. It consists of 12 highly Illumined Beings. Here are their names and the rays that they represent:

- Ray 1: The Great Divine Director

- Ray 2: The Goddess of Liberty

- Ray 3: Lady Nada

- Ray 4: Pallas Athena

- Ray 5: Elohim Vista, the creator angel

- Ray 6: Quan Yin

- Ray 7: Lady Portia

- Ray 8: Jesus

- Ray 9: Josiah

- Ray 10: Abraham

- Ray 11: Peter the Great

- Ray 12: Catherine of Siena

Of the 12 members, three goddesses have stepped forward to assist lightworkers to fast-track their ascension journey in order to free themselves for the planetary service they incarnated to undertake. They are Quan Yin, Lady Portia and Lady Nada, and we will ask for their divine karmic dispensations in meditation.

Visualization for Karmic Dispensation

1. Prepare a space where you can be relaxed and undisturbed. Light a candle if you can.

2. Sit quietly and breathe comfortably with the intention of petitioning the Goddesses of the Karmic Board for dispensation of karma.

3. Ground yourself by visualizing roots going from your feet deep into the Earth.

4. Ask Archangel Michael to place his deep blue cloak of protection around you. Be aware of his illumined presence as he surrounds you with his strength and pure love.

5. Invoke the magnificent fire dragons and ask them to release any dense, stuck frequencies. Feel their roaring flames dissolve everything that no longer serves you.

6. Once you feel bright and clear, call on the Goddesses of Karma with this invocation:

    'Beloved Goddesses of Karma, Quan Yin, Lady Portia and Lady Nada, representatives of the Divine Feminine for the Aquarian Age of Pure Love,

    I, [name], humbly ask you now for a karmic dispensation for [state your plea here]. [If you do not know what to request, the goddesses will be aware of anything that you need to clear.]

    I pledge in the name of the Light that I will use this freedom to activate fully my divine mission in service to All That Is.'

7. Within the crystal ball of your third eye the three Goddesses of Karma are now appearing.

8. Quan Yin, radiating beautiful cerise pink, takes your hand and starts to walk through a beautifully ornate garden with you. You feel calm, radiant and peaceful.

9. As you walk, Quan Yin asks what karma and circumstances you wish to clear. Mentally tell her.

10. You walk down some steps to a place where four seats have been set out. Lady Portia steps forward, radiating vibrant gold and the pure silver of grace, and indicates your seat.

11. Lady Nada appears, smiling, and says, 'Beloved soul, we have seen your life progress on Earth and we have watched you throughout every other lifetime, on and within many planets, galaxies and dimensions that you have experienced. Your service to Earth is exceptional and we have heard your request to have your karma dissolved. Your request has been granted to enable you to be free of restrictions, provided that your lessons have been learned to a sufficient standard for you to have this responsibility.'

12. Lady Portia stands up. She gently rests her hand upon the crown of your head. You feel a beautiful calming vibration running through you, right down to your feet. This vibration spreads through your physical, emotional, mental and spiritual bodies, through your aura and your fields, through the timeline of your current incarnation and through your ancestral karma, dissolving the conscious and unconscious acts of all those with whom you have shared bloodlines, through the acts of those into whose countries you have incarnated, through time and space, through all the experiences in all realities and universes that you have occupied since the moment of your soul's creation.

13. Sit quietly, aware of the silver light of grace running through every cell of your body. You may see this light very clearly.

14. Quan Yin stands before you, dressed in beautiful oriental robes. Around her shoulders is draped a pink dragon, peacefully asleep. She places her right hand over your heart and you feel the vibration of pure, unconditional love flooding through you, healing every facet of your being. Every single lower thought, word or deed is dissolved and forgiven by this incredible and beautiful flow of energy.

15. As she gently removes her hand, you feel the 33 petals of your heart chakra open like a pure white rose. You are aware that this energy has also transcended all time, space and realities that you have occupied.

16. The three Goddesses of Karma now stand. You do so too, feeling radiant and light as a feather.

17. As you thank them, they place their hands over their heart chakras to honour you and say farewell.

18. They lead you back up the steps and onto the pathway. You return alone, back to your sacred space.

19. Be aware of the magnitude of your sacred blessing. The goddesses have erased the karmic events from your Akashic records so that you can move lightly into the fifth dimension. You are free to serve, guided lovingly by your Higher Self. Every thought, word and deed can still create fresh karma for you, but you are ready to proceed into the Aquarian Age, working with the amazing team of light, making intergalactic history here on Earth.

20. With your eyes still closed, call upon Archangel Metatron to run his pillar of light down through your chakras into your Earth Star.

21. Ask Archangel Sandalphon to ground you firmly into Gaia and Hollow Earth.

22. Thank them both.

23. Open your eyes, gently stretch and smile. You have been set free on the road to mastery.

Step 40

Receive the Archangel Cloaks

Because the frequency of the planet is rising so quickly, Archangels Metatron and Sandalphon are delighted to offer special energy cloaks containing specific codes of light to those who are ready. All the high priests and priestesses who have ever lived are back in incarnation right now and if you have ever been one in any civilization anywhere in the world you can automatically receive these archangel cloaks if you ask for them.

If you have not been a high priest or priestess but nevertheless have an earnest desire to serve the world, your soul must decide if you are ready to wear these cloaks of light and power, so relax and trust that if you wish to receive them, it is right for you to do so.

The Metatron Cloak

As Archangel Metatron is the powerful archangel who is leading the planet into ascension, in order to wear the Metatron Cloak we must have done the basic groundwork for ascension. So we must have our 12 fifth-dimensional chakras open. Once we are wearing the cloak, it will keep them open. It will also confer protection from third-dimensional energies while we are in harmonic alignment with its energy.

When we are ready to wear this cloak in our energy fields, we will have a desire for service, so we will automatically help others on their ascension path. This entails empowering people so that they can see who they truly are and understand what they can do.

When we wear the Metatron Cloak, we will also be able to access Hollow Earth. We can enter the great crystal pyramid to connect to the four ascension planets, stars and galaxies, the Pleiades, Neptune, Orion and Sirius, and draw their wisdom into our energy fields.

The Gold and Silver Cloak

The Gold and Silver Cloak brings us into perfect balance, which is important for the ascension path. It balances our masculine and feminine high priest/priestess energy, our wisdom and power and our ability to give and receive and to make decisions in a truly balanced way based on intuition and fact. It brings us a sense of peace and feeling of personal empowerment. It also confers on us the courage to love. Once activated, our cloak will glow with the crystal pink aura of higher love.

When we are wearing it, we are magnetic to people, animals and situations. Consequently we are able to attract, for instance, the perfect home, the right partner or the job that aligns with our soul.

Wearing the Gold and Silver Cloak brings us into a higher frequency so that we are in tune and harmony with everything. This means that we can blend into our surroundings and even disappear when our energy matches that which is around us.

We can also attract angel sonics and use them to purify our space and people in our vicinity. Then anything becomes possible, for we enter the magic and mystery of the universe. We are able to place the cloak round others, or groups, so they too can feel the wonder.

Finally, when we wear this cloak, we can reach down into the seventh dimension of Hollow Earth to access the knowledge and wisdom of Earth. We can also reach up to the seventh dimension of the angelic realms for illumination.

Archangel Sandalphon, who is in charge of the Earth Star chakra, and Archangel Metatron, who is in charge of the Stellar Gateway, will together confer the Gold and Silver Cloak onto you in this meditation.

We have divided the journey to access these gifts into sections. You can do them individually or together.

Receive the Metatron Cloak and the Gold and Silver Cloak

1. Invoke the glorious Archangel Metatron with the words:

   'Beloved Metatron, I humbly ask and pray that you confer on me your golden orange Cloak of Ascension.'

2. Sit in a receptive position and you may sense or feel Archangel Metatron placing this cloak in your energy fields. Your aura is filling with golden orange light. See yourself blazing like a golden orange Sun.

3. Wearing your Metatron Cloak of Light, you are now ready to go on a journey to Hollow Earth, so relax in preparation for your journey.

4. Find yourself gliding down, deeper and deeper into the Earth.

5. As you enter the seventh-dimensional frequency you may be able to see the special light of Hollow Earth. Sense the peace and joy.

6. You may see representatives of different cultures or animals that are extinct on the surface, or even Lady Gaia's angels.

Entering the Crystal Pyramid

1. Ahead of you in the centre of Hollow Earth is a vast etheric crystal pyramid. As you approach it with wonder and respect, it glows with magical radiance.

2. Enter it and sit on a throne that awaits you in the middle of it. You are bathed in peace, safety, illumination and love. The high frequency of your

Metatron Cloak enables you to maintain in your energy fields the light codes that are about to be downloaded from the four ascension stars, planets and constellations of the Pleiades, Orion, Sirius and Neptune. Relax and breathe deeply as you prepare to accept this spiritual gift.

3. Become aware of a portal that leads to the Pleiades. Source sends healing directly to the Pleiades and the masters and angels of the Pleiades step it down to Earth.

4. A soft blue healing light pours down through the portal to envelop you. It fills your heart. All the light codes for perfect health and vitality are being downloaded into you now.

5. Turn your attention to the portal that opens through to Orion, the constellation of higher wisdom. Your energy fields may be programmed with information and knowledge that you are holding, waiting to use it in your life or to touch others with it. The Masters of Orion are directly in touch with the wisdom of Source. They can tell you whether and how you can use your knowledge for the highest good. Feel pure white light pouring through the portal from Orion into your soul star chakra, strengthening your connection with higher wisdom. Let this light flow into your aura, touching with Source wisdom all the keys and codes that you hold. Relax and know that your decisions will be guided by true wisdom.

6. Now focus on the portal that opens up to Sirius, where much of the higher knowledge of the universe is available. The spiritual technology for our glorious future is held here, waiting to be downloaded. Open yourself up to receive an input of symbols and light codes of higher knowledge and spiritual technology now.

7. Tune in to the portal that opens up to Neptune, the planet holding the higher wisdom, truth and light of Atlantis and Lemuria. All the keys and codes to the knowledge, wisdom, gifts and powers that were available then are waiting to be returned in the language of light into your energy fields now. The Masters of Neptune will activate them when you are ready. Golden Ascended Atlantis is now a step closer to you.

8. Your energy fields have received a great blast of light and empowerment. Relax as the light shower continues for a few moments.

9.   Receive blessings from Archangel Metatron and the Masters of the four ascension planets, stars and galaxies. Stay open to receive these. Stand in the glory of your true mastery.

10. Be very aware of your golden orange Metatron Cloak around you as you leave the pyramid in the centre of Hollow Earth. Thank Archangel Metatron as you walk through this seventh-dimensional plane and affirm that you will help and empower others onto the ascension path.

11. If you wish to stop now, sense yourself walking with joy and wonder through the seventh dimension. Then step your energy down until you find yourself in the place where you started. Or you may continue to relax in order to receive the Gold and Silver Cloak.

Receive the Gold and Silver Cloak

1.   You are now ready to accept the Gold and Silver Cloak from Archangels Metatron and Sandalphon. Affirm your readiness to wear this cloak:

     'Beloved Archangels Metatron and Sandalphon,

     I humbly ask and pray that you confer on me the Gold and Silver Cloak of perfect balance and magnetic attraction. I affirm that I will use its power for the highest good of all.'

2.   See, sense or imagine Archangel Metatron standing on your right-hand side and Archangel Sandalphon on your left.

3.   They are holding above you a sheet of gold and silver light that looks like shimmering silk.

4.   They gently drape this Gold and Silver Cloak over you and carefully stroke it into your aura.

5.   As it integrates into your energy fields, your heart opens, emitting a soft pink radiance. Breathe deeply as you light up.

6.   At this moment your energy is in total balance. Sense your light reaching up to the seventh heaven and down into Hollow Earth.

7. You are magnetic to your good. See or sense yourself attracting all that which is for your highest good. Take a little while to enjoy this.

8. Thank Archangels Metatron and Sandalphon for conferring the Gold and Silver Cloak on you.

9. Sense yourself walking in your Gold and Silver Cloak through the seventh dimension.

10. Then step your energy down until you find yourself in the place where you started.

You now carry in your energy fields the higher energies of the Metatron Cloak and/or the Gold and Silver Cloak. Use them with love and gratitude, as you are truly blessed. You are an emissary for the light.

You may do this visualization as often as you feel is necessary to reinforce the cloaks in your energy fields. At this moment they are protecting your higher light.

Step 41

The Higher Mahatma Energy for the 12 Chakras

In the era of Golden Atlantis, when the frequency was high and pure, many great beings and energies contributed towards a special pool of light. An analogy would be a group of people each contributing ingredients towards a huge fruitcake. Then they could all share the cake and be nourished by it.

The shared energy synthesized into a group consciousness of such a high frequency that it became known as the Mahatma, the great master, energy, or the Avatar of Synthesis. These are some of the energies it contains: the energy of the Buddha, the Christ, the Spirit of Peace and Equilibrium, the White Ascension Flame, the 12 rays, the Silver Ray, Metatron, the unicorns and the Goddess of Love. The Goddess of Love energy itself includes that of Quan Yin, Mary, Lady Nada, Lady Portia, Kumeka, Lanto, Lord Voosloo and Lady Venus. In addition it holds the Sphinx energy, which is the creative Godforce of this universe.

The Mahatma is the highest energy that we can currently access. It is stored by Archangel Metatron in the ninth dimension. It accelerates the path to ascension and helps to build the Antakarana bridge to Source. It was created in order to help us break up and clear unwanted mental, emotional or spiritual patterning and to keep the glands that govern our health and spiritual wellbeing strong and active. When we have a problem that needs to be resolved, the Mahatma raises our frequency in relation to it so that we rise above the challenge.

We can send this golden-white energy to others and if they are ready to use it, it will be wonderfully effective.

When the vibration of Atlantis devolved, this all-powerful high-vibration light was misused, so the pool was blocked off and we were no longer allowed access to it. At the Harmonic Convergence in 1987 it started to trickle back for our use. At the Cosmic Moment in 2012, we earned the right to open the floodgates and it is now pouring in at an even higher frequency, ready for us to invoke, use and bathe in.

Because it is such a special high-frequency golden-white light, the Mahatma energy is stepped down through our Monad so that it is perfect for our vibration.

We can use it to build our crystalline light body in preparation for the new Golden Age. By drawing it into our cells, we light them up and raise their frequency so that they can maintain the level of light needed for the glorious future.

When we draw the Mahatma energy down through our energy fields and physical body, it flows into the Earth, helping our planet to ascend. Please use it frequently, for it is very important both for our own ascension and that of the planet.

The Mahatma Energy and the Chakras

The higher Mahatma activates the 12 chakras. This is what it can do as it bathes each one:

The Stellar Gateway

Here the Mahatma activates and connects our spiritual brain patterns to our expanded cosmic master Higher Self and to All That Is.

The Soul Star

Here the Mahatma activates and connects our fifth-dimensional brain to enable us to remember our gifts and talents as a master.

The Causal Chakra

The Mahatma activates the fifth-dimensional brain to expand our connection and mastery to the world of spirit.

The Crown Chakra

Here our pineal gland absorbs the codes of light flowing to us from Source and containing the knowledge and wisdom of the universe that we are ready to receive. It also emits the light that builds our light body. It protects the structure of our DNA to honour our soul choices and maintain the codes for our spiritual gifts, talents and powers so that they can be available to us when we are ready. The pineal also keeps us in perfect divine harmony. Melatonin is created here to enable this spiritual energy to take form in the physical world.

The Third Eye

This is the location of the pituitary, known as the master gland because it sends out hormones or chemical messengers that control the working of many other glands, for example those concerned with urine production, growth hormones and the release of eggs. The pituitary is the gland of eternal life. When it is in perfect balance and harmony, we flow with cosmic abundance.

We can ask the Mahatma energy to reprogram this gland to release rejuvenating hormones to keep us physically, emotionally and mentally youthful. When it is in balance, we stay balanced.

The Throat Chakra

The thyroid gland, which is situated here, governs our metabolism and production of antibodies. The Mahatma energy can help this gland to balance our metabolism in a perfect way for our body, so that we are vibrant with energy. The parathyroid glands, which are also here, enable us to absorb calcium and balance the calcium levels to keep our bones, etc., strong and healthy.

On a spiritual level, when this chakra is in perfect harmony it allows us to tune in to all species and communicate with them telepathically. It also holds some of our powers from Atlantis.

The Heart Chakra
Our thymus gland, situated here, governs our immune system. When it is working in balance and harmony, we are strong, healthy and open-hearted. We can ask the Mahatma energy to balance our thymus gland and keep us vibrantly healthy.

The Solar Plexus Chakra
Here our pancreas deals with sugar and nourishment, physically, emotionally and mentally. It secretes insulin and digestive enzymes that enable us to absorb emotional and mental sweetness. When it is in harmony, we exude self-worth and wisdom. The Mahatma energy will contain vibrational aspects and imprints of higher wisdom from which we can benefit.

The Navel Chakra
Here the Mahatma energy helps to activate the fifth-dimensional ascended aspect of the reproductive organs, lighting up the creative force available to us. This aspect communicates with and draws in a new soul when it is time for parenthood. It holds the dynamic masculine force of the master builder. It also starts to put into place the keys and codes of manifestation triggered by our visualizations.

The Sacral Chakra
Here our gonads, ovaries and testes govern the sexual and reproductive organs of the body. The Mahatma energy stimulates our glands to help our sexual hormones to act in a perfect way and allow us to draw in transcendent love. If any of our glands have been removed, the Mahatma will work on the etheric ones to perform the same function.

The Base Chakra

At the lower dimensions this is where we respond to fight or flight situations. The Mahatma energy lights us up and empowers us to walk the path of trust and faith, spiritual discipline and bliss.

The Earth Star Chakra

In the Earth Star chakra the Mahatma energy helps us to ground and motivate our potential. It also activates our spiritual grounding to the planet, our connection to the heart of Lady Gaia. It helps us to bring back our fifth-dimensional blueprint, the divine vision of a perfect life.

Calling in the Higher Mahatma

1. Invoke the glorious Mahatma energy with the words:

    'I now invoke the Mahatma energy to flow through my body and my entire energy system to accelerate my ascension and that of Earth, allowing me to use my life in service to the divine.'

2. You may sense, feel or see a warm golden-white energy flowing down from your Monad into your Stellar Gateway chakra and filling the chalice.

3. Allow the beautiful golden-white to pour down into your soul star and fill it.

4. Let the Mahatma energy now stream into the causal chakra and fill it.

5. Let the Mahatma pour into your crown. Visualize your pineal gland like a small ball and allow the golden-white Mahatma energy to flow round it, relaxing it so that the ball becomes plump and full, balanced, energized and active.

6. Allow the golden-white light to flow down to the centre of your third eye, behind the bridge of your nose. Visualize your pituitary gland like a small ball and allow the Mahatma energy to relax it so that the ball becomes plump and full, balanced, energized and active. Mentally ask it to release hormones that rejuvenate you, allowing you to be physically, emotionally and mentally youthful, free and flowing. Visualize yourself full of health

and vitality, open-minded and accepting, happy, joy-filled and taking an enlightened perspective on all things. Open up to cosmic abundance.

7. Just relax now and focus on the centre of your throat. Visualize your thyroid gland like a small ball and allow the golden-white Mahatma energy to flow round it, relaxing it more and more. Sense it taking the golden-white light in so that it becomes plump and full, balanced, energized and active. Imagine the light radiating out to beings in all dimensions so that an exchange of communication can be established.

8. Allow the golden-white energy to move down into your heart chakra to strengthen your immune system. Sense your thymus like a little ball absorbing the golden-white light so that it becomes plump and full, balanced, energized and active. Sense your heart opening and radiating light and love to everyone. That radiation is becoming so strong that you are reaching out to connect with Venus, the Cosmic Heart.

9. Let the Mahatma energy course down into your solar plexus, surrounding your pancreas so that it becomes plump and full, balanced, energized and active in a perfect way for you. Feel the old being washed away as your deepest wisdom and self-worth start to reveal themselves. Have a sense of your true magnificence.

10. Let the Mahatma energy flood down into your navel chakra and sense the golden-white energy merging with your bright orange chakra, activating its potential at a higher level.

11. Sense the Mahatma energy merging with the pale luminous pink of your sacral. The light surrounds your reproductive glands so that they become plump and full, balanced, energized and active in a perfect way for you. It is activating and allowing transcendent love to fill this chakra.

12. Relax as the golden-white light fills your base chakra. Sense the energy surrounding your adrenals so that they become plump and full, balanced, energized and active, able to respond to challenges in a calm and clear way.

13. And now the energy moves down to fill your Earth Star chakra. Visualize your yin/yang symbol being surrounded and then filled with golden-white light.

14. It flows into the Earth to form a great pool of Mahatma light below you.

15. Let the Mahatma flow over and through your entire energy field, your emotional, mental and spiritual body. It is breaking up any old vibrations making higher possibilities available for you. It is building your crystalline body ready for the new Golden Age.

16. Visualize the Mahatma energy flowing to all parts of the world, breaking up the old and allowing the new paradigm to arise.

17. Visualize Earth surrounded in the golden-white light of the Mahatma.

18. Visualize the golden-white column of light forming a bridge from your Stellar Gateway to Source.

19. Invite the mighty Seraphim Seraphina to sing over you to anchor the Mahatma energy into you and your Antakarana bridge.

Step 42

Co-create the Aquarian Ascension Pool

The Intergalactic Council members were the architects of Atlantis and they worked through the high priests and priestesses, who were the master builders. There were 12 high priests and priestesses at any given time and they were known as the Alta. They took all the practical earthly decisions about the setting up of the continent while taking general instruction from the Council.

Thoth was a high priest in the first set to be appointed to Atlantis. He was also in the last set. The Intergalactic Council impressed the spiritual laws for Earth on him and they were finally encapsulated in the law 'As above, so below.'

The great high priest Thoth knew that our planet was extremely rich in metals and minerals, and that the metal within the Earth created a current that generated a magnetic field. Meditating in his temple of Amenti, he was shown the Earth as a crystal ball. Around the crystal ball were geometric pathways of pure gold, representing what were to become the ley lines of the planet. On each of the myriad crossing-points, a diamond was placed. The sphere was to be ignited with concentrated laser light.

Having received this vision, Thoth placed it in his amethyst crystal skull, from where it was passed to each of the crystal skulls held by the other high priests and priestesses. They held the vision with him until the ley-line system formed in the etheric.

Then the lines were imprinted into Earth by the Intergalactic Council, forming an energetic grid around the Earth.

The Alta would regularly combine their spiritual powers to perform magnificent feats of energetic prowess. They were experts at alchemy and manifestation and would always ensure that their creations were for the good of the whole. These covered a wide spectrum of services, from providing food to manipulating gravity in order to build incredible structures.

After the fall, this knowledge was taken to Egypt by the high priest Ra and used to build the Great Pyramid of Giza, which is a monument to the might of the Golden Age of Atlantis. Six cosmic pyramids were built in this way around the planet by the high priests and priestesses who brought the knowledge from Atlantis. Aphrodite oversaw the construction of the Mayan cosmic pyramid in Guatemala, which is still standing. The remaining four have been physically destroyed, but are energetically active. Zeus oversaw the building of the Tibetan one, Poseidon the Greek one, now under the Parthenon, Thoth the one now under Machu Picchu and Apollo the great pyramid in Mesopotamia.

During the Golden Era of Atlantis, many Illumined Beings contributed to the great pool of Mahatma energy that we can still access today. Archangel Metatron and Thoth have also now co-ordinated the creation of a new ninth-dimensional pool of light. Initially a group of dedicated souls, all of whom were high priests and priestesses in the Golden Era of Atlantis, formed a full Moon Healing Pool. Then every single archangel and many extra-terrestrials and masters added their light to it. A brand new form of energy was born: the Aquarian Ascension Pool. This is now held next to Archangel Metatron's ascension light above the Great Pyramid of Giza and is nurtured and looked after by Archangels Christiel and Metatron. Archangel Christiel sings over it to maintain its purity and high frequency. It has developed the colours of Archangel Christiel: milk white, rainbow and silver moonstone pearl.

The Mahatma and the Aquarian energy, although created in the same manner, vary in vibrational qualities. The Aquarian Pool will remain the responsibility of those who started it and will exist forever.

Working with the Aquarian Ascension Pool

The Aquarian Ascension Pool looks like an enormous lake, shimmering with moonlit rainbow light. Archangel Christiel constantly shines his light over it, holding it at a ninth-dimensional frequency, which maintains its liquid structure. It is truly magnificent to behold.

It is also beautifully simple to work with. To access it, as with all spiritual gifts and tools, all you need to do is ask. It can be used to boost personal light, open your chakras, clear psychic debris, help you with projects on your spiritual pathway and many other things. It can also be sent to other people and places. It is very powerful and if a situation needs to be changed, it will manifest a higher-vibrational alternative.

You can access it and add your energy to it by using the meditation given below. The full Moon is the most powerful time to do this.

Invocation to the Aquarian Ascension Pool

'I, [name], Child of the Light, invoke and integrate a full downpouring of the Aquarian Ascension energy into my fifth-dimensional crystalline matrix.
I allow my unified bodies, fields and merkabah to receive this blessing, radiating my divine ascended self in service to humanity, Gaia and All That Is. Now.'

Visualization to Access the Aquarian Ascension Pool

1. Prepare a space where you can be relaxed and undisturbed. Light a candle if you can.

2. Sit quietly and breathe comfortably with the intention of accessing and adding your light to the Aquarian Ascension Pool.

3. Ground yourself by visualizing roots going from your feet deep into the Earth.

4. Ask Archangel Michael to place his deep blue cloak of protection around you.

5. Invoke Archangel Christiel. Ask that your causal chakra be fully illuminated and connected to the angelic realms.

6. Visualize yourself sitting directly under a bright full Moon. The waters of a night-time lake lap gently at your toes.

7. As the waters touch you, they send sparkles of bright white light rushing through your body.

8. All around you, archangels and ascended masters are starting to gather by the water. They stand an arm's length from each other, as far as the eye can see.

9. You all raise your hands, palms upwards, and countless causal chakras illuminate as one, like 1,000 Moons. Energy starts to pour from your hands into the lake.

10. Watch as the lake lights up even more, becoming brighter and brighter as it fills with high-frequency energies.

11. After a short time, everyone stops. Bright white moonlit energy from the pool starts to surround you. Slowly and gently it enters your heart chakra and your chakras unify into a single column of light.

12. The light stretches from your Earth Star chakra below your feet, up through your base, sacral, navel, solar plexus, heart, throat, third eye, crown, causal, soul star and finally your Stellar Gateway. See it stretching up above your head, out through the cosmos, until it reaches the Great Central Sun.

13. Below your feet, your Earth Star sends out filaments of light, blending you with Mother Earth.

14. Ask the Aquarian ascension energy within you to touch, light up and illuminate anything that you wish to vibrate at a higher frequency.

15. Open your eyes, breathe deeply, and know that you have helped to co-create the most amazing light.

Step 43

The Mary Cloak

Universal Archangel Mary

Mary is a great Universal Angel who spans the universes spreading compassion, love, wisdom and healing. She commands the millions of angels who work with her to enfold with Divine Feminine qualities those who call on her.

'Mary' comes from the Latin word *mare*, meaning 'sea' or 'ocean', and Archangel Mary vibrates on a delicate Aquamarine Ray – *aqua* meaning 'water' and *marine* meaning 'of the water'. Water is the element that spreads love throughout the universes. It is in the atmosphere and in the cells of our body, as well as in the rivers and oceans, and Mary's love is everywhere in it.

In the Golden Era of Atlantis, Archangel Mary was seen in pure translucent aquamarine light. However, as the energy devolved, in order to reach the lower frequencies of humanity she made her light denser and appeared in a deeper, more opaque blue. She is now presenting herself in her lighter blue again.

Archangel Mary always travels with unicorns. A glorious team of these mighty beings lighten up and purify her path wherever she goes.

Mother Mary

Mother Mary, who gave virgin birth to Jesus, was a highly evolved, very pure initiate and master. She incarnated specifically for the purpose of giving birth to the being who would bring in the Christ Light for humanity. Her heart chakra was so open that the wondrous Archangel Mary, who overlit her during that incarnation, was able to shine her light through it. The result of this was that many people thought Mother Mary was an angel.

In Lemuria Mother Mary was known as Ma-Ra and became the first initiate of Lemuria. In Atlantis she was known as Isis and gave virgin birth to Horus. She was always seen with her beautiful, luminous, pure white unicorn.

Etheric Retreats

Both the Universal Archangel Mary and Mother Mary have their etheric retreats at Lourdes in France. Archangel Mary's retreat is within a globe of light from the ninth to the twelfth dimension, glowing from aquamarine to pure white. Here we are bathed at a cellular level in Divine Feminine love.

Mother Mary's retreat is ninth-dimensional and is like a castle with shimmering aquamarine-clad walls. Within it, millions of her angels chant the sound 'aah' to open hearts and touch everyone with love.

Whichever retreat you visit, you will be enfolded in pure love.

Both Mother Mary and Universal Archangel Mary comfort people everywhere. They succour the bereaved, the sad and lonely and help them to open their hearts so that they can embrace life again. They place blue light in the auras of pregnant women so that their babies will feel enfolded in love when they are born. Their blue energy also offers protection to the incoming soul. This special energy stays with the soul for about two years to give hope and encouragement.

Both Marys send their angels and unicorns to help children who are in need of love and support and respond to the supplications of mothers who are concerned for their children, even when the children are adults.

If a soul needs help to pass into the light, you can call on Mother Mary or Archangel Mary, for they and their angels will take the spirit and conduct them to the other side in a caring and loving way.

Universal Archangel Mary's Cloak

When your heart chakra is open and fifth-dimensional, it can connect to the Cosmic Heart. Then, if you ask, the Universal Archangel Mary will place her pale translucent aquamarine cloak, filled with the energy of love, compassion, empathy, wisdom and healing, into your aura.

In order to receive this, you must undertake to touch and enfold others with these energies. When you wear the Mary Cloak, you can work with Mary and assist her mission, for you will develop huge etheric wings of light. This will enable you to spread the blessing of the Divine Feminine on Earth.

So, if you are ready and you wish to receive the Mary Cloak, you can ask the unicorns to touch and open your heart, then ask Archangel Mary to place her Mantle of Aquamarine Light into your aura.

Receive Universal Archangel Mary's Cloak

1. Prepare your space, ground yourself and call in Archangel Michael's blue cloak of protection.

2. Find yourself resting under an azure sky in a beautiful valley where there is a waterfall cascading down through rocks and green ferns.

3. Allow yourself to relax in this peaceful place. Feel your bare feet on the grass and let your toes uncurl as they let go.

4. Mentally call in a unicorn. Be aware of a beautiful pure white horse with a horn of spiralling light moving peacefully and gently towards you.

5. The unicorn lowers its head towards you and light from its horn touches your heart. Sense it opening.

6. Now invoke Archangel Mary with these words:

'Beloved Archangel Mary,

I humbly ask and pray that you confer on me your aquamarine cloak of love, wisdom, compassion and healing. I affirm that I will spread its light to others and anchor the Divine Feminine energies here on Earth.'

7. Be aware of the great archangel, surrounded by hundreds of angels and unicorns, approaching you. You may hear angels singing as they approach.

8. The great angel is looking at you with infinite love and joy. Her bright blue eyes see your soul and she loves you unconditionally.

9. She enfolds you in her soft and beautiful wings. Let her shimmering pale aquamarine light fill your aura totally.

10. She strokes the light into your energy fields, forming a soft silky cloak around you.

11. Take a moment to feel the beautiful cloak and breathe in the love and wisdom you have been given.

12. Thank her.

Giving Healing with Mary's Cloak

1. Focus on the back of your heart centre and sense aquamarine light flowing out and forming wings. Sense them growing bigger and bigger as more energy streams from your heart.

2. Imagine you now have vast aquamarine wings, which unfurl and spread out. Take a moment to flap them.

3. Enfold people in need to comfort and heal them. Through you these people will be touched with Mary's light.

4. Let your wings become even bigger so that they can span your town, state or area. Enfold every person and animal in this area. Sense them softening and relaxing into the safety of your wings of light.

5. Allow your wings to become so light and enormous that they can spread over your whole country. Let the love and wisdom touch the hearts of politicians, bankers, business people, hospitals, schools or any other organization. Sense any lower energies dissolving and being replaced by higher love.

6. And now your wings are reaching out across the world, getting bigger and bigger. Let the love and wisdom, compassion and healing touch the hearts of world leaders, those who run international businesses and organizations or take decisions that affect the whole planet.

7. Send the Mary light to touch every animal and bird in the world, bringing them love, healing, comfort and hope, and to touch the hearts of all people so that they respect and honour animals.

8. Let the Mary light flowing through your heart touch every marine creature in the ponds, lakes, rivers and oceans, bringing them love, respect, healing, comfort and hope.

9. Let the Mary light flowing through your heart touch every tree and plant in the world, encouraging them and filling them with love.

10. Visualize a column of aquamarine light forming in front of you. It reaches from Earth to the heavens and at the base an elevator appears. Ask that any stuck souls, whether human or animal, who need assistance to pass be brought here by Archangel Mary's angels.

11. You may be aware of many angels bringing souls to the column, where they are entering the huge cosmic light elevator. Surrounded by Archangel Mary's angels, the elevator is rising up like a ball of light, taking many people and beings with it, back home with love.

12. As you spread the light of Mary's cloak, be aware of the balance of the world changing from masculine to feminine, to love and peace, and of that change bringing about the new paradigm.

13. Now you are an ambassador of love and healing, one whose energy can change the world.

Step 44

Tools for Prosperity and Abundance

Huge changes are hitting our beloved planet. This is the first time that such evolution has ever occurred so quickly and we all have to *be* while this happens.

The chemistry for this is beautifully simple. For this transformation to take place we have to relax and trust that the universe will provide for our earthly needs, so the keywords are 'Let go and let God.' At the same time, however, we have to be responsible for our higher energy.

Money and abundance, which includes all that our heart desires, are big lessons for many of us now on Earth. The frequency is changing and the flow of energy that represents abundance, both in terms of finance and happiness, is changing.

In the fifth dimension we are a master and are expected to send out a frequency that will provide a pure universal return. This means we must provide for ourselves. This is critical for the fifth dimension. Until our frequency is pure, we may be sending out mixed messages to the universe.

Here is an example of how this works. You have been living in a cottage (third dimension). You have added extensions (fourth dimension). Now you want to build a mansion over it. However, you still live in the old construction until you have demolished it completely and finished the bigger build.

Manifestation is our birthright. It is incorporated in our fifth-dimensional blueprint and it is time to access it now. The archangels have given us two powerful tools to assist with this process: Huna prayers and Archangel Raphael and Merlin's Prosperity Template meditation.

Huna Prayers

While we are building the new we can call in expert help in the form of Huna prayers. They are a very effective manifestation tool and directly communicate wishes to Source, in positive terms, in order to provide the prosperity and abundance we require. The results can be miraculous when used with pure intent. Our process is supervised by Archangel Raphael.

Huna prayers are thousands of years old and were created by the Kahuna Indians when they moved to Hawaii following the fall of Atlantis. They wanted to pull in a purer flow of light to give them the abundance they needed to build a new life and the high priest Hermes 'remembered' this method of manipulating energy into a higher form.

Because a Huna prayer powerfully shapes the cosmic flow, it must be used with great integrity.

A Huna Prayer for Abundance

Here is an example of a Huna prayer for abundance. You can alter it in any way you like as long as the wording is positive. You will need to say it aloud with force and pure intention daily for 30 days. At the end of each prayer, sit with your palms up to receive the divine blessings you have commanded.

'Beloved Archangel Raphael and Divine Source,

I, [name], Child of the Light, ask from the centre of my glowing heart for the immediate provision of divine abundance in the form of [request].

I fully rescind my previous limitations and personally open myself to my God-given gifts from Source.

I fully open myself to my limitless power of manifestation to provide access to my Source mission.

In the name of Beloved Source, I fully accept and gratefully receive all that is now provided for me.

Thank you.

It is so.'

Repeat three times.

Then say once:

'My beloved Higher Self,

I now request from the centre of my glowing heart that you impart this request to Source, along with my fully activated power of manifestation.

It is so.'

Breathe this prayer to Archangel Raphael and Source, using the full power of intention.

Sit with your palms open upwards and state loudly:

'I now command the Rain of Blessings to fall.'

Because the energy has speeded up, you may find you receive your blessing before 30 days. If you have not received it by the time you finish your Huna prayer, stop saying it. Give the universe time to work on your command. If it still does not attract what you asked for, meditate on this to discover any reason within you. It may be that the universe has something much better waiting for you!

Merlin, the master magician, and Archangel Raphael have offered assistance to co-create the change needed. Here is a meditation for you:

Archangel Raphael's and Merlin's Prosperity Template Meditation

1. Call upon Archangel Metatron to light up your Stellar Gateway. It is bright gold.

2. Call upon Archangel Mariel to illuminate your soul star. It is radiant magenta.

3. Call upon Archangel Christiel to light up your causal chakra. See it glowing luminous moon-white.

4. Call upon Archangel Jophiel to pour liquid gold into your crown.

5. Call upon Archangel Raphael to touch and activate your emerald third eye.

6. Call upon Archangel Michael to light up your electric blue throat chakra.

7. Call upon Archangel Chamuel to activate your pure white fifth-dimensional heart centre.

8. Call upon Archangel Uriel to illuminate your golden solar plexus.

9. Call upon Archangel Gabriel to touch and activate your bright orange navel, your soft pink sacral and your bright platinum base.

10. Finally, invoke Archangel Sandalphon to light up your swirling deep grey Earth Star.

11. Next, invoke the pillar of ascension light from the core of Helios. See it come down through your open and activated chakras.

12. As it does so, invoke the Aquarian Ascension and Higher Mahatma energies to fuse with it.

13. As you reach the sacral and base, invoke Ascended Master Merlin and Archangel Raphael.

14. Ask them to remove the poverty consciousness template from these chakras and turn them into higher light.

15. Feel this energy lift from your chakras, leaving them pure and clear.

16. State out loud three times:

    'I, [name], declare myself free of any poverty consciousness agreements, templates or realities, from this lifetime or any other.

    I vow, in the name of the light, to attract pure abundance to myself and my planet.'

17. Visualize yourself joining hands with Merlin and Archangel Raphael and invoke the golden fire dragons of Lemuria.

18. Spin the energy from the old paradigm of the collective consciousness clockwise round the planet, increasing in speed.

19. Watch as the fire dragons turn this energy into a higher light.

20. When this is done, repeat the process anticlockwise, still linked with Merlin and Raphael.

21. Finally, see the same energy being gently lifted from the sacral and base chakras of every soul living on Earth.

22. See their 12-chakra system light up with their ascended colours.

23. With Merlin and Archangel Raphael, place a new golden halo of fifth-dimensional prosperity and abundance around the Earth. This is a pool of energy to which everyone will have full access. All are One.

24. Thank Merlin, Archangel Raphael, the fire dragons and yourself.

Step 45

Heart Healing from the Pleiades

The Pleiades are a seventh-dimensional ascended star cluster known as the healing stars. As with the other ascension planets, stars and galaxies intimately connected with Earth, there are 12 masters, highly evolved beings, in charge of the energy here.

The great Archangel Mary, who steps through Venus to bring love, compassion, empathy and the Divine Feminine pink light, also steps through the Pleiades to touch people with her aquamarine-blue-heart healing energy. She overlights Mother Mary and if you call on the Archangel Mary or Mother Mary they will bring whatever energy is appropriate for you.

The Blue Pleiadean Rose

The Masters of the Pleiades draw pure blue heart healing energy directly from Source into a vast blue etheric rose which acts as a transformer down to their seventh-dimensional energy. They then access this energy to use with wisdom and discretion, distributing it to places and beings where they deem it is needed. They do this in loving service.

The blue rose has 33 petals like the human heart, the number of the Christ consciousness. Its centre is pure white Source light.

People who originate from the Pleiades or step their energy down through that star cluster carry healing in their auras. The animals and insects that come to Earth from the Pleiades also carry part of this blue healing light in their energy fields so that they can spread it once they have incarnated.

The spiritual technology used by the Pleiadean light beings is beyond anything we can currently comprehend on Earth. The blue rose is a sacred geometric tool that can be used for many purposes, including healing, and one of these is to enable us to clear our chakras and accelerate the rate of their spin.

Medical Assistance

The Pleiadeans are currently overlighting the acceleration of the blueprint of medical knowledge here on Earth as we move into a fifth-dimensional frequency. By 2032 the entire system will have evolved beyond our current recognition. All healing will be soul healing, as it was in the Golden Era of Atlantis. Vibrational healing will be applied to anything that is not of soul perfection and this will affect the physical body.

The Pleiadeans can step down to the third dimension through the electrical current we use. They can then affect the flow. They are currently operating through medical equipment if they are asked to do so. For example, if someone is on a kidney dialysis machine and healing is invoked for them for the highest good, the Pleiadeans will be able to reach them through the electricity in order to raise their frequency.

In the Golden Era of Atlantis, power was harnessed by passing sunlight through pyramid-shaped crystals into copper tubing. This was done with the co-operation of the elementals, who aligned with the crystals. The electrical power thus produced was a very high frequency and the Pleiadeans used this to hold the original divine health blueprint of a person.

Working with Computers

If you ask for assistance to harmonize your energy fields with the vibration emitted by your computer or phone, the Pleiadeans will do this.

Working with Crystals

Quartz crystals are a perfect conduit for the Pleiadeans to bring through their energy. You can program a quartz crystal with the Pleiadean rose so that it can be placed on the body and activated when needed. The deva of the crystal will record the frequency of the information so that it can be used whenever the keeper of the crystal wishes.

The blue rose in your Earth Star chakra provides a permanent link to Hollow Earth by sending down blue roots. It provides a single unified column of blue healing light up your chakra system, through your Stellar Gateway and Monad and into your Antakarana bridge. When this is fully operational, it enhances your connection to the Pleiades.

Visualization to Connect with the Pleiadean Rose

As with any spiritual gift, we have to invoke the blue Pleiadean rose. Then the angels of the Pleiades will place it in our chakras. Because the rose is a powerful healing tool the angels of the Pleiades suggest you start by asking for one to be placed in your heart chakra. Here it will spin as it takes in as much of the Pleiadean healing energy as you can accept. You may feel it flowing from your heart down your arms to your hands and then you can touch any part of your body that needs it or you can pass it on to others. When your body has adjusted to the rose in your heart, you can ask for one to be placed into your other chakras.

1. Prepare a space where you can be relaxed and undisturbed. Light a candle if you can.

2. Sit quietly and breathe comfortably with the intention of connecting with the blue Pleiadean rose.

3. Ground yourself by visualizing roots going from your feet deep into the Earth.

4. Ask Archangel Michael to place his deep blue cloak of protection around you.

5. Tune in to the Masters of the Pleiades and ask them to hold you in a blue ball of light.

6.   Invoke the Pleiadean rose and visualize it in front of you.

7.   Ask for it to be placed in each one of your 12 fifth-dimensional chakras and relax as this is done.

8.   Visualize the blue light merging with the golden orange of your Stellar Gateway. This will automatically start to heal your divine connections, mending any breaks in your energy pathways to Source. This means that if any rungs of your Antakarana bridge are broken, the Pleiadean energy will mend them so that you can reach up to the Great Central Sun.

9.   Visualize the blue light merging with the magenta of your soul star. This will send healing to your soul connections, both your ancestral links and people still in incarnation.

10. Visualize the blue light merging with the white of your causal chakra. This will soothe your connection to the world of spirit and act as a beacon, attracting angelic energy to you.

11. Visualize the blue light merging with the crystal gold of your crown chakra. The blue healing light will flow through the petals of your thousand-petalled lotus and start to heal the universal connections from here.

12. Visualize the blue light merging with the crystal green of your third eye. Here the rose stimulates clairvoyance by healing anything that was blocking the perfect activation of this chakra and enables you to communicate with beings from other planetary systems.

13. Visualize the blue light merging with the royal blue of your throat chakra. Here it activates truth through perfect verbal resonance. It also enables you to heal through your words and communicate with other species.

14. Visualize the blue light merging with the pure white of your heart, so that healing radiates from you at all times unless you consciously switch it off.

15. Visualize the blue light merging with the gold of your solar plexus. It raises the frequency to a fifth-dimensional level and holds it, so that you are in touch with your essence of confidence and self-worth.

16. Visualize the blue light merging with the orange of your navel chakra, so that you really can welcome and accept all beings. With the rose in place, when your navel blazes welcoming masculine energy, it also radiates a gentle feminine healing light.

17. Visualize the blue light merging with the pink of your sacral chakra. The blue Pleiadean rose prepares this chakra to bring in transcendent love. This adds beautiful healing energy to all your relationships.

18. Visualize the blue light merging with the platinum of your base chakra, spiritualizing it and enabling the fifth-dimensional frequency of bliss to be anchored here.

19. Visualize the blue light merging with the black and white of your Earth Star chakra. Now see it become a unified column of brilliant blue light reaching down into Hollow Earth and up to the diamond core of the Great Central Sun.

20. Thank the beings of the Pleiades.

Step 46

The Spiritual Laws to Activate Alchemy and Magic

In the Golden Era of Atlantis, the high priests and priestesses passed communications from the Intergalactic Council to the Magi, so called because they could perform magic, in other words manipulate the properties of the universe by understanding the spiritual and physical laws. They were highly evolved shamans. The information the high priests and priestesses wished to transfer was downloaded from the Great Crystal in the Temple of Poseidon to individual temple crystals. The Magi of each temple would go into deep trance and draw the information from the crystal, then pass on what was appropriate to the people.

The training of the Magi involved mind control and this enabled them to practise magic in the form of levitation, telekinesis, teleportation and manifestation. They were taught to use the frequencies of sound and light and to heal. Finally they were taught to fly and communicate with other galaxies. This involved awesome spiritual discipline and control of their thoughts and emotions.

They used their great power wholly in service to the people and it was the purity of their devotion that enabled them to maintain their power. It was only when one of the Magi used the energy of the Great Pool of Atlantis for his own personal use that the great civilization started to implode. Purity of intention is the essential ingredient of true alchemy and magic.

Magic and miracles start in the spiritual and higher mental realms, and the energy filters down to the physical, where it creates an alchemical reaction. For example, whenever we follow our intuition and take appropriate action, we are aligning with divine truth, and that is when miracles can happen.

The greatest alchemist of all time was St Germain, who also had an incarnation as Merlin. He understood the great immutable spiritual laws and was able to activate them to practise magic. He was very aware that all energies were interlinked and had to be used for the highest good. When working magic, anything lower is returned to the sender multiplied, while pure love showers blessings on the giver.

We can invoke the assistance of St Germain and Archangel Zadkiel to hold us, other people or situations in the Cosmic Diamond Violet Flame of transmutation. By dissolving the old, this enables us to reach into the higher levels to create magic and miracles.

Archangel Gabriel, pure white angel of purity and clarity, is in charge of the navel chakra, where our higher creative powers are held. When our intention is right, he shows us how to unlock our door to inspired creativity, and this is another key to magic and alchemy. Our creative visions trigger a response from the universe that allows physical manifestation to take place.

Opening the Door to Miracles

Whenever we let go of self and do something for the highest good of someone else, we are opening the door to miracles. When we envision the divine perfection of another, our pure vision can help to bring about that renewal. If a healer sees their client as divinely whole, wonderful healing can take place. When our heart feels pure compassion for someone in distress, our love creates divine chemistry within them to bring about physical and emotional transformation. This is spiritual law in action.

When we send genuine positive loving thoughts to someone, we are lighting them up with fifth-dimensional energy. This raises their frequency and enables them to feel safe. Then they can relax at a deep cellular level. This then allows miraculous attitudinal changes to take place. This applies whether we are talking to someone, massaging them or giving them healing.

Every seed contains the divine blueprint of the flower it can become. Certain physical things, such as water, light and nutrition, are required in order for this perfection to blossom, but there is something else too. If we hold the vision of the perfect outcome for the plant in all its glory, our pure energy will create an alchemical reaction within it that will enable it to fulfil its greatest potential. The elementals will step in and help to bring this about. Plants, trees and other sentient beings all respond to pure love.

The same is true about the way we treat ourselves. Tests show that our very DNA reacts to positive energies we send to ourselves. It stretches out, relaxes, connects the codons and allows us to be in touch with our sacred gifts and talents. The entire chemistry of our body changes and even deeply entrenched karmic and genetic patterns transform as we become a master of miracles and magic.

However challenging a situation may be, when people working in unison envision the highest possible outcome, an alchemical reaction takes place allowing good to happen. Then everyone pulls together so that, miraculously, they experience oneness. This was one of the secrets of Golden Atlantis.

There are certain qualities that allow miracles to take place. Truth, faith, unconditional love, integrity, honesty, honour and other fifth-dimensional qualities are some of them. These transform the energy of the universe.

The Alchemy of Relationships

Part I

1. Take time to relax, ground yourself and place a cloak of protection round your aura.

2. Think of someone who is not generally popular. It may be a neighbour, work colleague, fellow club member, parent at your child's school, relative or even a stranger.

3. Invoke Archangel Gabriel to pour pure white light over you and Archangel Zadkiel to hold you in the Violet Flame.

4. State your highest intention to envision them in divine perfection.

5. Picture them as glowingly healthy and happy.

Part II

1. For the next 21 days treat them as if they are popular, liked, appreciated and respected.

2. Greet them with a big smile as if you really value them.

3. Note the change in your attitude and theirs.

4. At the end of 21 days, extend this practice to others.

Healing a Situation

1. Take time to relax, ground yourself and place a cloak of protection round your aura.

2. Think of a situation that needs to change.

3. Invoke Archangel Gabriel to pour pure white light over the situation and Archangel Zadkiel to hold it in the Violet Flame.

4. State your highest intention to envision the situation transformed into divine perfection.

5. Use your creative imagination to visualize a harmonious outcome for all concerned.

Step 47

The Christ Consciousness Portals

As our planet ascends, a very specific energy change is occurring. Moving from third-dimensional reality to fifth-dimensional reality in such a short space of time requires a great deal of energetic, structural and alchemical manipulation. Most of this work is being carried out in the higher realms by constructing a blueprint of the new reality. This is then applied to the energy of our existing planet and this creates the necessary changes.

According to the Intergalactic Council, the initial construction has been completed. Archangel Metatron and the dedicated team working with him have brought Earth into a fourth-dimensional reality. So the third-dimensional world is being collapsed and overlaid with a higher frequency. As this process speeds up, so will the awakening of souls on Earth. Every single sentient being on Earth is now living in a higher stream of light. The true groundwork for this started when Jesus incarnated. As he ascended, he opened a golden portal of Christ consciousness, allowing the new higher structures to start integrating with Earth's denser energy.

Many of the ascended masters in spirit have been very focused over the last 2,000 years on keeping this flow of energy moving. With Archangel Metatron and the ascension team they have been feeding Christ consciousness energy into the third-dimensional ley-line grid at specific points all over our planet. These are the 33 sacred cosmic portals that all started to open at the Cosmic Moment in 2012 and will continue to pour increasing amounts of glorious Christ Light onto the planet until 2032.

Using Numerical Codes

Archangel Metatron has offered information to assist this process further. Numerical codes to activate smaller Christ consciousness portals were released, with the intention of allowing lightworkers to create their own portals of high-frequency Christ Light. This is a very powerful gift and is only granted following consultation with the Intergalactic Council.

Using these ancient numerical codes, a soul carrying a high vibration of love and integrity can now use these portals.

There is an initial code that activates the Christ consciousness merkabah within an individual. This is 13-20-33. When stated with intention, this number attunes Christ Light straight into the four-body system. It will energize that system and light up the aura and the fifth-dimensional merkabah with pure Christ Light.

The second code is 12-22-33. When stated with loving intention, this activates a portal of Christ Light at the location chosen by whoever is using it. This method is beautiful, gentle and very powerful, as it immediately raises the frequency of everything around it.

Permission from the Intergalactic Council should always be sought prior to using the second invocation. It is an energy which has an instant effect wherever it is applied.

Visualization to Create a Christ Consciousness Portal

1. Prepare for meditation. You are about to undertake high-frequency work for yourself and your planet.

2. Invoke Master Jesus of the Intergalactic Council and tell him that you intend to use the Christ consciousness portal with the highest integrity. He will now watch over you as you work.

3. Sit quietly, eyes closed, and say the words:

   '13-20-33, Christ consciousness merkabah, activate.'

4. Your body and fields will immediately be filled with pure golden light. You are connected directly to the pool of the Gold Ray of Christ. Breathe this energy into your entire being.

5. Visualize your fifth-dimensional merkabah expanding around you, lighting up everything it touches.

6. Visualize a place to which you would like to add Christ Light. It may be your own home, somewhere near to you or a place far away. The energy will work there immediately.

7. State:

   '12-22-33, Christ consciousness portal, activate.'

8. See a spot of pure intense golden light illuminate your chosen area.

9. Ask the mighty Archangel Christiel and Master Jesus to expand this light and gently introduce it to the existing vibration.

10. See everything it touches light up with pure unconditional love.

11. Ask that your portal becomes a fully open gateway for the energies of the Christ consciousness.

12. Invoke the golden Lemurian fire dragons to guard it and maintain its integrity at all times.

13. Thank Master Jesus, Archangel Christiel and the golden dragons.

14. Open your eyes and smile. You are a co-creator with the divine, assisting the heart chakra of our planet with the Christ consciousness portal.

The Heart Chakra of the Earth

Glastonbury, UK, is the heart chakra of our planet. It is through here that the higher realms are pulsing the most intense frequencies into the planetary matrix. Work has already been done to ensure that the flow remains high, pure and clear. The more souls that focus on this, the faster the energy will move.

Visualization to Spread Light through the Planetary Heart Chakra

1. In meditation, take a few moments to visualize Glastonbury Tor.

2. See pure golden light flooding from the Cosmic Heart down through the Tor and into the planet.

3. Watch this light spreading in golden lines from this point into a beautiful six-pointed star around the base of the Tor.

4. See this light expanding further into the ley lines and into a web of bright gold around our planet.

5. To anchor this flow of energy into the planetary heart chakra, say:

   '12-22-33, Christ consciousness portal, activate.'

6. Invoke the mighty fire dragons and the legions of Archangel Michael and Anubis to maintain the ascended integrity of Glastonbury at all times.

7. Thank them, open your eyes and know that you have assisted with the divine plan on Earth.

8. Energize this vision with positive, happy, beautiful thoughts.

Step 48

Carry the Pure White Light and Ascension Flame

Pure white light contains all colours. When we carry this light in our aura, we are totally at peace. This means we are harmless and therefore completely safe. Nothing and no one can touch or hurt us.

There are several mighty pure white beings or energies who radiate this light into the energy fields of Earth. We can invoke any or all of them to enable us to take in white light at a cellular level. It will be absorbed into our mental, emotional and physical body when we are ready. Here are some of the beings:

Lord Maitreya

In 1956 Lord Maitreya became Lord of the World. He draws love directly from Source and steps it down through the Cosmic Heart to those whose lights are on. As overlord of the entire solar system, including Earth, his task is to raise the consciousness of humanity to open it to the Universal God Mind so that we can move gloriously through the new Golden Age.

He is the head of the White Brotherhood and Order of Melchizedek, which hold and spread pure white light. He incarnated on Earth to bring in the Buddha energy so that people could access the fifth, sixth and seventh dimensions. Since 2012 those who are ready have been able to access the ninth dimension. He also incarnated as Krishna.

It was Lord Maitreya who overlit Jesus while he carried the Christ energy and on the cross. Currently he is helping those who are bringing in spiritual technology for the future and is activating the healing of the world.

You can connect with him in meditation at his etheric retreat at the Confucius Temple in Beijing, China. Ask him to hold you in the Christ Light and open you up to carry more of it. He will also place Christ Light in your solar plexus to fill it with peace and a sense of personal empowerment.

Lord Melchizedek

Lord Melchizedek is known as the Eternal Lord of Light. He is a group energy that holds the Christ Light as well as the ancient wisdom for this universe and receives teachings directly from Source. Abraham, Moses, Elijah, David and Jesus were high priests in the Order of Melchizedek and incarnated because there was a need for their light on Earth.

You can connect with Melchizedek in his etheric retreat above Guam, in the Pacific Ocean, to receive cosmic teachings.

Archangel Gabriel

Archangel Gabriel is the pure white angel who helps to bring clarity and purity to all situations and people by cutting through illusion and taking them into higher dimensions. The concretized representation of his energy on Earth is the diamond, which symbolizes purity, eternity, clarity, truth and honour.

The Unicorns

These high-frequency pure white beings who resonate between the seventh and ninth dimensions bring love, enlightenment, joy and soul purpose to those they touch. Their horns are a spiral of light from their third eye. When they shower us with pure white light, they offer miraculous blessings.

The White Ascension Flame of Atlantis
The pure white ascension flame was created in Golden Atlantis. It holds the highest frequencies for the blueprint of the ascension process and contains the keys and codes of eternal light and peace. Serapis Bey is the Keeper of the White Flame. If we are ready, supported by Archangel Gabriel, he will hold this flame in our energy fields.

The Universal Angel Butyalil
The mighty Universal Angel Butyalil radiates a pure white light. He is in charge of the movement of the cosmic currents, including our personal cosmic flow, and works with the Seraphim Seraphina. He also helps us to see and accept our magnificence, enabling us to ascend into higher frequencies. He will link us to the Intergalactic Council so that we can personally present petitions for the light, as outlined earlier.

We can connect with the Universal Angel Butyalil at his retreat above Earth in the central point where the four ascension planets, stars and constellations, Neptune, the Pleiades, Orion and Sirius, meet. He steps down through the pyramids of Egypt so we can also ask to meet him in the etheric above the Great Pyramid.

Carrying Pure White Light
The following visualization will bring pure white light into your body and fields if you relax and allow it to be absorbed. It will offer you the opportunity to become a co-keeper of the White Ascension Flame and to serve the Order of Melchizedek.

Visualization to Carry Pure White Light

1. Relax, ground yourself and place Archangel Michael's cloak of protection around you.
2. Surrender into the softness as Archangel Gabriel enfolds you in his pure white wings.

3. A pure shimmering white light is approaching and your beautiful unicorn steps out of it. He is radiating peace, love and joy and tilts his head to pour sparkling white blessings from his spiralling horn of light all over you. Be still and accept them.

4. Archangel Gabriel lifts you gently onto the unicorn and you rise swiftly through the many dimensions of the inner planes until you see a pure white Palace of Peace ahead of you.

5. As you land in the central courtyard you become aware that the gardens are filled with cascading white scented flowers. Step off the unicorn and smell the blooms.

6. Serapis Bey approaches, dressed in white and carrying the pure White Flame. The flame expands and becomes huge as Serapis Bey places it over your energy fields and illuminates you.

7. Archangel Gabriel lifts you back onto your magnificent unicorn and sits behind you as you travel through the cosmos to the place where the four ascension planets and stars meet above Earth.

8. Here the vast pure white Archangel Butyalil awaits you. Just being in his presence fills you with white light and helps your life to flow more peacefully.

9. Archangel Butyalil holds up a vast cosmic mirror. You look into it and see, consciously or unconsciously, your magnificent, expanded, cosmic self.

10. Archangel Gabriel and the unicorn travel with you back to the place where you started.

11. Here Archangel Gabriel places his glittering, shimmering diamond over your energy fields.

12. You are pure white light.

Step 49

The Golden Flame of Atlantis

The Golden Flame of Atlantis has been kept in the etheric by the wondrous Archangel Metatron. It is a mighty tool used specifically for transforming new areas of land into places of high frequency.

Atlantis was originally a vast continent filling the Atlantic Ocean. It rose and fell five times over the period of its existence. Each time the land emerged from the sea it was new and refreshed, but it became progressively smaller in area and a different shape whenever a new experiment was attempted. The format also changed with each new trial. Technology had to be redeveloped, structures built again and ways and means of living spiritually pulled out of the etheric and into the physical world. This was supervised by the Alta, the senior priesthood, under the direct guidance of the Intergalactic Council. Patience, dedication and perseverance were required and it was only during the fifth and final experiment that fifth-dimensional living was achieved for a period of 1,500 years.

This was a huge breakthrough, proving that such purity could be developed in everyday life simply by adhering to the spiritual Law of One. This was the primary law of Atlantis, consisting of the basic principles of 'As within, so without; as above, so below.'

The Golden Flame of Atlantis was gifted to the Alta during the second experiment. Raising the vibration of the land by personal frequency alone was not enough, so the Alta were given tools to help them to survive and also to manipulate matter to suit their needs.

The Golden Flame, handed to Ra and Thoth via Lord Voosloo and Archangel Metatron, was put to use immediately. Applied to the land and waters by direct invocation, it raised and held the atomic and energetic substructure of certain areas at the chosen octave of the fifth dimension. The ley lines were then lit up and activated in harmony with this energy. After this process, established power points were brought into alignment too. The land was then gridded with massive quartz crystals. This kept the frequency of the chosen places high by harnessing the solar energies, so that they became the harmonious land stretches of Atlantis.

Once this work had been done, each high priest and priestess was given a facet of the Golden Flame to use at their discretion. It became a vital tool, along with the many other spiritual gifts, to keep everything in harmony.

By the end of the final experiment, the continent of Atlantis had split into five separate islands. The Alta occupied the Isle of Poseida, on which stood the great Temple of Poseidon. Life on the other islands was very varied and some areas were no-go zones even for the mighty Alta, who had once held Atlantis in a golden light for all. They actually became hostile towards the Alta, creating the template for the divisions and boundaries that we still experience today.

The forces at play were much more powerful than those we currently experience and so barriers had to be erected to maintain the pure vibrations wherever possible. The Golden Flame of Atlantis was used to mark out zones of high frequency to protect them from energetic corruption. Bright blue flags with an emblem of the golden flame marked these regions and high-frequency beings bravely holding the light knew that they were safe within these areas.

As well as this important work, the Golden Flame of Atlantis was versatile enough to use on resources such as food. All food in Atlantis, particularly Golden Atlantis, was blessed to keep it as pure as possible. It would literally glow with light.

Using the Golden Flame

Very recently, as the vibration here on Earth has risen, so has the level of responsibility for lightworkers. The walking Masters of Earth are the souls leading the wave of ascension. They are at the forefront of the changes and are bringing through the stored tools and information. The Golden Flame of Atlantis was returned in November 2013 and is now available for use again. It was put to global use immediately and sent round the planetary water system in a water blessing ceremony, so that the seas of Earth sparkled and radiated pure gold.

This ancient Golden Flame is extremely powerful and is being dispensed under the authority of Archangel Metatron. Here are some ways in which you can invoke it and use it to help our planet:

- Invoke Archangel Metatron, Thoth and Lord Voosloo to place the Golden Flame within your fields. When this happens you will carry this vibration and pass it to everything around you via a cellular chime.

- Send the Golden Flame to areas that you know need to be illuminated. It will work on energy structures that need changing, such as political or educational systems.

- Bless water, food, land, trees and plants with this energy.

- Visualize the Golden Flame spreading around the planet. This will spread the Christ consciousness energy flow to everything that it touches.

- Program crystals to activate the Golden Flame in specific areas. This can be your own home, places you are visiting and even buildings such as hospitals.

- Water systems are a potent way to spread this amazing energy. Use the exercise below to increase the Golden Flame of Atlantis on Earth for the higher good of everyone.

Visualization to Use the Golden Flame of Atlantis

1. Prepare a space where you can be relaxed and undisturbed. Light a candle if you can.

2. Sit quietly and breathe comfortably with the intention of working with the Golden Flame of Atlantis.

3. Ground yourself by visualizing roots going from your feet deep into the Earth.

4. Ask Archangel Michael to place his deep blue cloak of protection around you.

5. Pick your favourite meditation spot at home or outside near a stream or river.

6. Choose a rock or crystal and place it in flowing water, perhaps a stream, ocean or waterfall.

7. Call upon Thoth, king and high priest of Atlantis, and the archangels who work with him.

8. Thoth and Archangels Metatron, Gabriel, Michael, Raphael, Uriel, Zadkiel and Jophiel join you and pour high-frequency light over you. Other archangels and masters may also surround you. Honour them.

9. Bless your crystal with love and pure intention and ask the beings with you to do the same. Visualize it glowing with a multitude of frequencies. See these merge into a golden glow containing dappled lights within it.

10. Place your rock or crystal within your chosen water source. Ensure that the water is moving. Close your eyes and imagine the cloud of gold filling every molecule of liquid.

11. Invoke the Golden Flame of Atlantis. Ask it to ignite the ancient energies and illuminate your golden cloud further.

12. See your water light up at a bright sun-like frequency.

13. The energy starts to move rapidly now. Visualize it flowing through your water system, joining the rushing rivers and moving out into the open sea.

14. Once it has reached the sea, watch it spreading faster and faster until it has enveloped the whole planet.

15. Sit, breathe deeply and see all the waters on our planet as gentle, golden and fifth-dimensional. Know that this energy will be carried to every outlet, every home and every single soul living on Earth.

16. Open your eyes, knowing our planet has been truly blessed.

Step 50

The Gold Ray of Christ

Christ consciousness is an energy of unconditional love. It forms a golden ray of light which can be used by anyone for a number of purposes. It carries love, wisdom, healing, protection and the ability to illuminate anyone or anything with a much higher frequency. When invoked, the Gold Ray of Christ is drawn at a ninth-dimensional frequency from the pool of Christ consciousness held in Sirius and steps down to the level at which it is needed. However it cannot lower its vibration below the fifth dimension, so whenever we receive it, we are bathed in fifth-dimensional light.

This ray carries unconditional love. This is love that totally accepts the recipient exactly as they are. When we radiate total non-judgement and acceptance, it melts all barriers and self-doubts in the person to whom we are sending this energy. This enables them to see and feel everything from a higher perspective. It also opens their heart centre and unlocks their gates to abundance consciousness. Consequently they become more relaxed, generous and giving. When we carry this light within us, we touch people profoundly. It can also be sent to people or places to raise the frequency of any situation and is a wonderful gift to share.

The Gold Ray of Christ is a very protective energy. If we have worked with it in any other lifetime, it will already be within our auric light codes and programmed to protect us totally. If we are using it for the first time, it will soon establish itself within our energy fields with the assistance of Archangel Christiel.

When we have the Gold Ray of Christ in our aura it takes all the energies in our vicinity into their highest aspect. It will attract high-frequency energy to us and keep our fields in resonance with our Higher Self. It carries the wisdom of Christ consciousness, which allows us to take decisions from a higher perspective about relationships and circumstances of all kinds.

Christ Consciousness and the Opening of the Earth's Heart Chakra

After the fall of Atlantis, the amount of Christ Light on Earth diminished dramatically and continued to do so until the Intergalactic Council formed a plan. The great initiate Jesus was sent to Earth on a special mission to raise the level of Christ consciousness on the planet. With great difficulty he did so and at the same time reactivated the Gold Ray of Christ so that it could pour onto Earth again through the portal created by his ascension.

Recently the Christ consciousness inflow has been dramatically increased by the opening of the heart chakra of the planet in Glastonbury, UK. The geometry of the sacred ley lines surrounding Avalon, which is an old name for Glastonbury, now resonate in harmony with the fifth-dimensional crystalline matrix placed around the planet. This is enabling the Illumined Beings to establish permanent Christ consciousness on Earth, thus affecting the open-heartedness of all ascending beings. This is the first time this has been achieved since the Golden Age of Atlantis. Instead of being part of an experiment, as it was in Atlantis, Christ consciousness is now a permanent fixture on Earth.

The Christ Light vibrates at the frequency 33. Just saying the word '33' attracts the Christ Light to you. If you add another 3, making 333, it intensifies the energy.

Each of the 33 cosmic portals that started to open on the planet at the Cosmic Moment in 2012 carries a level of Christ Light plus other individual qualities. As these portals open, they are spreading ninth-dimensional heart energy through the ley lines and the ethers, establishing the fifth-dimensional planetary merkabah.

In some places the heart energy, which desires freedom, love and equality, has opened people up more quickly than the political system of their country allows. This has sometimes led to conflict with the existing way of being. It has forced brave souls to face difficult initiations, but will ultimately allow the Christ Light to flow there more freely.

In other places on the planet, the establishment of Christ Light is a far gentler process and is working in harmony with the divine ascension plan.

Many people are increasingly aware of Orbs and other energies appearing in their photographs and this has drawn our attention to the fact that any soul who has ever incarnated on Earth is accompanied by an angel or by the Gold Ray of Christ. The reason for this is that once you have had experienced Earth in a physical body you feel compassion for others. Because of this, as you travel in your spirit body, you may try to help someone on Earth and thus prevent them from learning their lessons. This applies even to the greatest masters. So an angel or the Gold Ray of Christ is sent with all spirits to ensure they do not interfere in anyone's karma.

Invocation to the Gold Ray of Christ

To invoke the Gold Ray, say:

'I now invoke the Gold Ray of Christ for my complete illumination and protection.'

Repeat three times.

Visualization to Send a Ball of Christ Light

1. Prepare for meditation by relaxing and grounding yourself. The Gold Ray of Christ will protect your aura.

2. Invoke Archangel Christiel and Master Sananda. Ask them to access the highest level of the Gold Ray of Christ for you.

3. Visualize this glowing pure gold frequency pour down from the ninth-dimensional pool of the Gold Ray of Christ.

4. Feel it come down through your Monad and gently filter through your higher soul body, illuminating it with pure unconditional love.

5. The Gold Ray of Christ now enters your Stellar Gateway, opening and activating it fully. It flows down through your soul star, your causal chakra, your crown, your third eye, your throat and your heart. Here it rests momentarily.

6. Feel it expand until the 33 petals of your heart are fully open.

7. It then streams down through your solar plexus, navel, sacral and base chakras and finally into your Earth Star below your feet. Your 12-chakra system is now open, glowing and flooded with pure Christ Light.

8. Hold your hands in front of you, palms facing each other.

9. Visualize the Gold Ray of Christ flowing from your open heart, down your arms and out of your hands.

10. The energy starts to form a ball. Pour more energy into this, expanding the width of your arms and hands, until the ball is as large and powerful as you wish it to be.

11. Release it with love and intention and send it to a situation, person or animal that you wish to bless.

12. See Archangel Christiel carry the ball of the Gold Ray of Christ away and place it gently upon your intended spot.

13. Open your eyes and know that you have sent out a beautiful and powerful blessing.

Know that you are loved and protected at all times and carry the Christ Light within your four-body system, aura and merkabah.

Step 51

The Wisdom of Trees

Archangel Purlimiek, the angel of nature, oversees the trees in the world, while the elves help to look after them.

Trees are ancient sentient beings who were birthed on our planet from the heart of Source. They hold the codes of divine love within their essence. In addition every single tree is graced with a particular quality with which to help humans, animals, elementals and insects. When we sit or stand within the aura of a tree, the sacred geometry of these qualities is downloaded into our aura and our frequency is raised by harmonic transference. If we open our heart to the tree and absorb its energies, we will feel subtly different.

People intuitively recognize, for example, that sturdy, solid oak trees carry strength, courage, endurance and fortitude. You will receive these qualities if you stand under an oak tree. If, at the same time, you invoke Archangel Michael and bring his deep blue light down through the tree into yourself, this will enhance the power that comes to you from the oak tree. If you need extra strength or courage, stand in warrior pose with your heels firm and flat on the ground under an oak tree, then sense Archangel Michael's blue energy flowing into you and imagine yourself conquering the situation. If you cannot find a physical oak tree, visualize one!

Trees keep records of local history, while forests are keepers of ancient wisdom. When we are ready, they will impart relevant information to us.

Occasionally a special specimen that is planted alone grows into a huge and powerful being radiating such presence that it holds the entire area within its majesty and light. For example, huge cedar trees are still seen that dominate and grace an entire estate. These trees will protect and empower those within their energy field and give them a sense of belonging to something greater than themselves.

Beech trees heal by opening people's hearts to forgiveness. If you invoke Archangel Chamuel and visualize his pink energy pouring down through the beech tree into the roots, love and heart healing will spread through the tree root network, even if the trees are some distance apart. Then anyone drawn to them will feel nurtured by their benevolence.

You can do your part by invoking and visualizing any high-frequency energies flowing down through trees. This will enhance the individual tree and the area. For example, you can activate the Cosmic Diamond Violet Flame through a tree in woodland and your offering will spread until it transmutes all lower frequencies in that wood.

You may also like to bring the Christed Mahatma, the Gold Ray of Christ, the new ascension rays or any of the archangel energies down through a tree and cause this light to spread.

Qualities of Trees

Yew trees have always been planted in cemeteries or sacred places because they place psychic protection round the space. Then spirits can rest in peace and sacred places can maintain their light without interference.

The other tree that valiantly defends those who live within its protection is the hawthorn. It may be small and sometimes scruffy, but it is powerful. If you own a house or a farm with a hawthorn hedge, bless the hawthorn and thank it. It is working very hard to keep lower energies away.

Here are some of the other qualities offered by trees:

- *Ash:* This elegant tree carries Divine Feminine qualities.

- *Chestnut:* This bountiful tree teaches us abundance consciousness and invites us to play.

- *Elm:* These sensitive trees help us to stand in our power in a balanced way.

- *Fir and Pine Trees:* These trees help to regenerate us and lift our spirits. They will raise our frequency if we let them.

- *Holly:* This prickly tree teaches us to understand that people are behaving badly because of their own hurt and encourages us not to judge them.

- *Mahogany:* This glorious tree offers reliability and trust.

- *Plane:* This is a very sensitive tree that can tune in to human frailties. It merges its energy with ours and then raises the frequency to help us feel better.

- *Poplar:* This tall tree teaches dependability and reliance.

- Silver Birch: This delicate tree helps to open our heart.

- *Willow:* This lovely tree teaches us about flexibility and how useful this can be.

Fruit and Vegetables

The fruit of a tree contains its seed, its life force or essence, and often concentrated nutrients. This not only nourishes, it also brings the gift of the tree into our cells. A banana brings wisdom, an apple health, a chestnut prosperity and common sense, a cherry love, an orange joy, a strawberry happiness, a pear calm.

In the natural scheme, every fruit and vegetable is designed to be ripe when most needed by the indigenous humans and animals.

Forests

Forests are the lungs of our planet. Through photosynthesis they oxygenate the world. Oxygen is the element that carries the light of Source throughout the universes. The glory of the Great Divine Plan ensures that every sentient being breathes in oxygen, even fish, who extract it from water through their gills. Every breath that we take brings Source light directly into our cells. At the same time, the very air contains droplets of water carrying divine love. So when we breathe fully, we take in Source love and light. The more deeply we breathe, the calmer and more connected we feel. Babies, who are still linked to Source, automatically take in huge slow breaths.

Walking in forests helps us to regenerate and heal because we are renewing our connection with Source. Trees, especially pine trees, bring us into the fifth dimension if we are ready.

Forests also draw in and store light from other star systems or planets. For example, the Black Forest in Germany is connected to Jupiter and its ascended aspect, Jumbay. Here are held many keys for future healing and ways of balancing people, animals and the planet. Currently allopathic medicine has a purpose, because deeply entrenched karma has meant that imbalances in our body have become extreme. When we step off the wheel of karma, we will return to the naturally provided methods of healing that keep our systems in balance. Many of these are provided by trees.

Many forests in South America are connected to Venus and are holding higher codes of love to enable the natural world to live in unimaginable harmony and joy.

The world is changing and rising in frequency very quickly. The divine plan includes Australia being reforested as soon as this continent learns to control the climate and command the rainfall. These yet-to-be planted forests will draw in huge amounts of knowledge about spiritual technology and wisdom to enable Australia to help the whole world.

Because so many trees are currently being felled all over the planet, those that are left are having to work very hard. They sometimes feel tired and unappreciated. When you send them love, it strengthens them and enhances their ability to pour out unconditional love.

Visualization to Connect to Trees

You can do this exercise under a physical tree or visualize it. Either way you are tuning into the energy of trees.

1. Prepare a space where you can be relaxed and undisturbed. Light a candle if you can.

2. Sit quietly and breathe comfortably with the intention of connecting to the tree kingdom.

3. Ground yourself by visualizing roots going from your feet deep into the Earth.

4. Ask Archangel Michael to place his deep blue cloak of protection around you.

5. Be aware of a shimmering blue-green glow around you as Archangel Purlimiek enfolds you in his wings of light. Relax into them.

6. He takes you to a tree. It may be enormous or tiny, but you are aware it has something to offer you.

7. Open your heart and tune in to your tree. Sense its aura.

8. As you sit or stand under it, the sacred geometry within its energy fields is enhancing your own fields. Relax and allow this to happen.

9. What qualities is the tree offering you? Sense these lighting up within you.

10. The tree may have a direct message for you. Accept it, consciously or unconsciously.

11. You may be aware of an elf sitting on the branch of the tree watching you.

12. Thank him for being there and enjoy the connection.

13. Thank the tree and Archangel Purlimiek.

14. Open your eyes.

Step 52

Expanding the Fifth-
Dimensional Heart

When your fifth-dimensional heart is open and glowing, it is the most magnificent sight. This is the moment your archangels have been waiting for since the golden years of Atlantis. They see a bright white light within which the 33 open petals radiate your personal ascension frequency while the golden cord in the centre links gloriously to the Cosmic Heart and then right through to Source.

The fifth-dimensional heart is the template for the ascension process. The entire chakra system is based around this central point. Once it is active, it lights up the other chakras until they are totally clear, rather like a self-clearing high-performance engine. This does not mean that the lessons contained in the other chakras are automatically cleared, however, for this only happens when each one evolves.

As already mentioned, Archangel Chamuel is overseeing the opening of the first 10 petals of the heart and the early ascension initiation process. Now that so many people are opening their hearts, Archangel Christiel, who holds the light of the causal centres, is overseeing the activation of the higher heart within the ascension process. He is pouring pure Christ Light into the ascended hearts of those who are ready so they may spread this energy to others. The cellular chime of this opens the hearts of increasing numbers of spiritual aspirants who are drawn to this frequency.

At the summer solstice of June 2014 there was a massive heart activation via Glastonbury Tor, the heart centre of Earth. This was sent out on the merkabah Christ consciousness frequency, 13-20-33. Those who were involved radiated powerful frequencies, enhanced by the solstice energies and Archangel Metatron, to provide a global heart-opening trigger.

Many similar activations are now taking place around the world all the time. These are hastening the opening of our glorious heart chakras to bring the world into alignment with the higher crystalline grid.

The New Golden Grid

Until 2012 Earth was still functioning with the ancient system of ley lines that was laid down at the start of Atlantis by Thoth. At the Cosmic Moment, Archangel Metatron slowly and carefully turned down the frequency of the old planetary grid.

A new liquid gold one is now being fed into a higher-frequency structure of ley lines round the planet. As the liquid gold ley lines are once again envisioned into place by lightworkers under the guidance of Thoth, Archangel Metatron is taking the energy and establishing the new sacred geometry.

This is one important example of how lightworkers and the angelic forces are co-creating the new paradigm.

The new grid is becoming a crystalline web of light that is a much higher frequency than the old one. Higher information will be passed through this newly created network and as the planet evolves this crystalline grid will become the permanent ley-line system of Earth. When this happens, physics, mathematics and the magic of pure alchemy will merge. Then our knowledge and understanding will be completely reformed.

The information we had in the Golden Era of Atlantis has been stored ever since in a number of different places and formats. Special and sacred parts of it are in each of the 12 crystal skulls and the Sphinx. The angels of Atlantis and the angel dolphins hold some of it. Much is stored in the Halls of

Amenti, the learning halls in the inner planes, as well as in the great crystal pyramid of Hollow Earth. All of the knowledge is programmed into the thirteenth skull, the amethyst crystal skull of Atlantis. Golden Atlantis was the foundation for the new Golden Age that we are approaching now and when enough people's hearts are fifth-dimensional, this information will once again become available to birth the new world at a higher level.

As the new higher crystalline grid is energetically placed round the planet by the Illumined Masters and the archangels in charge of the ascension process, people's hearts will literally burst open with joy as a surge of love pours round the planetary grid. Souls living on Earth will witness miracles on a daily basis to accelerate this process.

This energy can no longer be ignored and will soon be igniting everyone's heart centre. This phenomenon has been predicted and we are being asked to look for miracles within the madness.

Visualization for Opening and Expanding the Fifth-Dimensional Heart

1. Prepare a space where you can be relaxed and undisturbed. Light a candle if you can.

2. Sit quietly and breathe comfortably with the intention of opening and expanding your fifth-dimensional heart.

3. Ground yourself by visualizing roots going from your feet deep into the Earth.

4. Ask Archangel Michael to place his deep blue cloak of protection around you.

5. Focus on your heart centre and visualize it glowing pure, radiant, white and swirling.

6. Call in Archangel Chamuel, Archangel Mary and Archangel Christiel.

7. Ask Archangel Chamuel to touch, open and illuminate the first 10 petals of your heart. As he does so, feel them unfurling and filling with pure love. Your heart is starting to glow brightly.

8. The beautiful Archangel Mary, angel of the Divine Feminine, touches your heart centre. Breathe in deeply and exhale slowly as the seven petals of your mid-heart open in unison. The light from your heart now takes on a magnificent powerful glow. White and pink light pours from you, swirling into your surroundings.

9. Archangel Christiel is with you, pure lunar white. He touches the 16 petals of your higher heart and it opens fully.

10. Breathe in deeply and exhale slowly, watching the luminous white light flowing from your chest. It is the colour of the Cosmic Heart itself.

11. Take time to breathe this glorious light out to people, animals, places and situations. Let your light embrace them and raise them to a fifth-dimensional frequency.

12. Visualize a pure white column of light leaving your chest. It travels up, continuing through your higher chakras and your monadic presence, out into the vastness of the cosmos.

13. A white pillar of light is pouring from the ninth-dimensional Cosmic Heart towards you. This light infuses with yours and you become one with this infinite pool of Source love.

14. Visualize your open heart surrounding the Earth with love. Imagine every soul on the planet glowing as you are. See yourself becoming one with them.

15. Open your eyes, thank the archangels and spread blessings.

Step 53

Discover Your Own
Ascension Ray Energy

You may be familiar with the ray colour that represents your personal spiritual energy, gifts and talents. As you are now ascending and expanding your energy bodies, this ray colour is changing. Archangel Metatron is offering you a new, higher colour vibration with which to work. It can be anything on the colour spectrum – red, blue, green, pink, orange, yellow or anything that comes to you. You will be attuning to the ray energy of your Higher Self.

The other mighty being who can help you discover and attune to the ray of your Higher Self is Lord Voosloo. He will enable you to tune in to your highest aspiration on your journey to ascension.

To help you to connect more deeply to Lord Voosloo so that he can facilitate the new connections, we are including a little about him here.

Lord Voosloo
Lord Voosloo comes from another universe to help us at special times of spiritual acceleration on the planet. He was a wise one of Mu. Later he incarnated during the Golden Era of Atlantis. He was the highest-frequency high priest to incarnate during the entire period of Atlantis, one of the few beings from the eleventh dimension that has ever taken a body. Now he has returned to

help bring back the glorious vision of what can be within a vast universe. He holds the great flame of universal possibility. To enable these aspirations to take shape, he is helping to keep us all in balance, mentally and spiritually.

Because Lord Voosloo understands all about Atlantis and has an overall perspective on what occurred, he can connect us to the deepest wisdom of the Golden Era. He also assists us to balance our 12 chakras so that we can bring back our 12 strands of DNA.

Currently some babies are being born with 12 strands of DNA, but they can't be activated because the atmosphere is too low. Because of this, some of them are withdrawing part of their soul energy and presenting as autistic. Often they can be helped by their family keeping their energy high and clear. Also, the unicorns may help by reconnecting these children's soul energy if they are willing. It is really helpful to call on Lord Voosloo and the unicorns to keep the energy round these special souls pure, light and balanced, so that they can fulfil their potential. There may only be a few such children now, but the numbers will increase rapidly as 2032 approaches.

The Ninth Ray

Lord Voosloo is here to help us and our planet ascend graciously. Recently he has become very proactive with the ascension process. He is working closely with Serapis Bey and Archangel Metatron. Working together as a powerful team, they are creating the ascension templates for humanity and the higher atomic crystalline structures for Gaia. These crystalline structures are layered over the existing third- and fourth-dimensional energies so that they amplify new Christ consciousness energies and pour them into the planet. At present this process is taking place continuously.

Lord Voosloo has become the master of the Ninth Ray, the Yellow Ray of Harmony that returned to the planet in 2001. It carries the keys, codes and sacred geometry of human harmony, world peace and co-operation with joy. When Lord Voosloo shines his Yellow Ray into our mind, energy fields and chakras, it lights up the desire for accord, unity consciousness and harmony that is held within our fifth-dimensional blueprint. His light will help to bring about the balance and equilibrium the world needs in order to move smoothly into the new Golden Age.

We can ask him to keep us in balance so that we stay on our golden ascended path.

Connecting with Lord Voosloo

Lord Voosloo's etheric retreat is above Stonehenge. The portal of Stonehenge is only partly open but will be fully open by 2032. It is seventh-dimensional and takes you into your seventh-dimensional light body. Then you will see the world from a much higher perspective and comprehend the workings of the universe. You will see through eyes of love as if you are an angelic being.

Lord Voosloo works at a very high frequency. To prepare yourself to visit his retreat, eat lightly, relax and be aware of his light forming around you during the day.

Visualization to Visit Lord Voosloo at His Retreat

1. Prepare a space where you can be relaxed and undisturbed. Light a candle if you can.

2. Sit quietly and breathe comfortably with the intention of visiting Lord Voosloo's retreat to discover your personal ray energy.

3. Ground yourself by visualizing roots going from your feet deep into the Earth.

4. Ask Archangel Michael to place his deep blue cloak of protection around you.

5. Visualize yourself sitting in the centre of the circle at Stonehenge.

6. Invoke Archangel Metatron and Lord Voosloo.

7. Archangel Metatron steps forward and takes you from the centre of the circle down a flight of beautifully lit steps into an ornate chamber. Gold light flows all around you. Breathe this into your cells.

8. Lord Voosloo approaches you, smiling. He wears bright orange robes, with the emblem of a Sun on his chest. He invites you to take a seat on a beautiful golden chair.

9. Archangel Metatron stands behind you, beaming pure ascension light.

10. Close your eyes, bring your attention to your third eye and see what colour comes to you. The first one that you see will be your primary ray colour.

11. Allow this colour to flood through every cell of your body. As you do so, energy pours from your Higher Self through your crown chakra, lighting up your third eye.

12. Lord Voosloo is standing in front of you. He has a ball of bright energy in his hands. What colour do you see? This is your expanded ray energy and Lord Voosloo is handing it to you now.

13. Take a few moments to hold this ball of coloured light in your hands. Notice how it feels. Sense its vibration and how powerful it is.

14. Take this ball of coloured light and place it within your heart centre. Feel it expand through every molecule of your being into your aura, your fields, and out into the area around you. It expands until it fills your fifth-dimensional merkabah and can extend for 32 kilometres (20 miles).

15. You now have your ascended ray colour. This is your energy to work with, the colour of your Higher Self.

16. Thank Lord Voosloo and Archangel Metatron and leave the chamber with love and gratitude.

17. Open your eyes and feel your new expanded power.

Step 54

Ascension Crystals and Crystal Skulls

Humanity's affinity with crystals goes back to the pre-Atlantean civilization of Lemuria. During this period the quartz and crystal template of our planet was forming in the third dimension. Massive geographic changes took place everywhere, creating vast underground beds under intense heat and pressure.

The Lemurians knew the effect that these conscious non-sentient formations would have in the future years. They gathered Source energy through the Cosmic Heart and with it they mixed divine qualities from the aura of Earth and many other stars, planets and constellations. They programmed this energy with high-frequency spiritual knowledge and information and focused this ineffable light into the ley lines of Earth, where it solidified, and so the Lemurian crystals, with their awesome power and energy, were formed.

Lemuria passed and Atlantis was born. During this period the crystal resources were utilized in everyday life, from simple communication to the highest peaks of technology ever used on Earth. Now, aeons later, in harmony with the planetary awakening, crystals and their spectrum of power have become a focus of attention again.

As the planetary frequency rises, more souls are becoming aware of this source of natural power and spiritual enhancement and the information stored away within crystals is starting to activate. Every single rock, stone and grain of sand has a vibration and the capacity to store information. Modern-day technology uses silicone in the circuit boards of computers, and science is starting to realize just how much further this can and will benefit humanity in the future. As stated by the Masters of Atlantis, the fifth-dimensional world will be powered by these crystals, and this time is drawing very close.

On a personal level, most lightworkers are drawn to a type of crystal that resonates with their frequency. Some are attracted simply by colour and clarity, others by knowing the specific vibrational properties of each crystal and how it can enhance their personal development. For example, it is widely known that the beautiful violet-coloured amethyst contains a calming and protective frequency that resonates with the Violet Flame, while sugalite is associated with the deeply protective energies of Archangel Michael and passes these frequencies to those that use it, and rose quartz calms, soothes and connects to Archangel Chamuel.

A beautiful grade of quartz is also becoming widely used, called ascension quartz. This is quartz of the highest and purest clarity and it is utterly flawless.

Crystal Skulls

During the very high-frequency Golden Era of Atlantis, crystal skulls were used by everyone. Their shape was chosen by the high priests and priestesses in consultation with the Intergalactic Council, as the skull represented the consciousness, the intellect and the personality of humans. Every home on the Atlantean continent contained a skull that was tuned into the master frequencies of the temples. These in turn were linked to the Great Crystal in the Temple of Poseidon on the Isle of Posieda.

These skulls acted as methods of communication, computers and a link to the flow of higher information from the

Intergalactic Council. People were taught to fashion their own skulls in crystal workshops, connecting their own energy deeply to the companion skulls they were creating.

Later in this fifth-dimensional period the experts learned how to blend different forms of crystal together, giving their skulls a range of frequency and power that was suited to individual needs and requirements. For example, if an aspiring soul wished to improve their ability to connect with their psychic powers, they could fashion their skull using the purest grade of quartz. Then, using the advanced methods of laser cutting, together with specific sound frequencies and mind control, an emerald would be placed in the third eye of the skull. This represented the expanded third eye of its owner. Another example would to blend pure liquid gold into the crown of the skull, reflecting a higher flow of Source energy.

These skills, together with deep love and knowledge of this craft, have now been brought through at a soul level by the crystal workers of modern times. As the doors open to the higher realms, skull makers are intuitively working with increasing power, turning raw materials into beautiful creations that reflect the perfection achieved in Atlantis.

At the turn of the century amazing discoveries were made and crystal skulls made from different types of quartz have now revealed themselves to humanity. The majority of these discoveries were made in South America and the skulls were predominantly fashioned from clear or smoky quartz. Only one has appeared made of pure amethyst. The archaeologists who discovered these artefacts realized that some of them were ancient beyond all historical records. They are now being kept in museums or by chosen keepers who are assigned to guard them as they come to life and reveal their secrets.

Spiritually, people are drawn to them and upon communicating with them realize that they have access to a flow of higher knowledge. Crystal skulls have once again become tools and are becoming popular as people tune in to these higher frequencies.

A crystal skull fashioned by a craftsman is a companion, a record keeper and a valuable asset for many souls on the spiritual path. Many use them to tune in to the ancient energies available to assist them in remembering who they truly are.

Programming Crystals

All crystals and crystal skulls are programmable. A piece of simple quartz is capable of holding a vast amount of information. Archangel Metatron used to direct the crystal technologies of Atlantis and is once again assisting with this process. His energy can illuminate, activate and guide anyone wishing to enhance their crystal connections.

Exercise to Program a Crystal or Crystal Skull

1. Start with a piece of clear quartz. Because of its clear and neutral vibration it is the easiest and clearest crystal to program.

2. Cleanse your crystal under running water. Leave it out in sunlight or moonlight and surround it with the Cosmic Diamond Violet Flame.

3. Connect with the deva of your crystal. All crystals have an elemental being that looks after their frequency. Ask the deva to activate your crystal for programming.

4. Invoke Archangel Metatron and ask him to fill your crystal with pure ascension light. This will enhance its power massively and connect you more closely to it.

5. Ask Archangel Metatron to place any other specific energies he wishes to into the crystal.

6. Pick a favourite meditation that you use regularly.

7. Hold your crystal in your right hand and set your intention to program it.

8. Say your meditation aloud as you normally would.

9. When you have finished, ask the deva to place this information into your crystal as an active recording. State that you wish to access this regularly.

10. Ask Archangel Metatron to place his energy around the crystal to enhance and protect your information.

11. Your crystal is now programmed and you can activate it whenever you wish. This is quick, easy and convenient.

12. Remember to cleanse your crystal regularly, especially if you carry it with you.

13. Thank the crystal, the deva and Archangel Metatron for their service.

Step 55

The Instant Sun

Here is another powerful ascension activation and a tool to keep your energies clear. The Instant Sun is pure etheric fire that burns away any dross in your energy fields. It is extremely powerful and versatile and is perfect for keeping your own individual frequency pure and clear, particularly if the vibrations round you are mixed. If you choose to activate it, you can make it large or small as appropriate and it will remain in place until it is turned off or collapsed. It can be expanded as far beyond yourself as you wish. You can even use it to encompass the planet.

Thoth was particularly adept with energetic tools and their application and the Great Atlantean Master Voosloo gifted the Instant Sun to him. It is a chakra-based energetic instalment or device that is used around a person or an object. As its name suggests, it is Sun or Helios energy that, when activated, creates a ninth-dimensional ball of light frequency around the activator.

This technology is a gift and will only be dispensed to those who intend to use it for the purposes of assisting themselves and the development of the planet. Masters Voosloo and Thoth are presenting this to you now, as you are one of those who has accepted the responsibility to do your part to help the world to ascend.

As the new Golden Age dawns, the spiritual gifts we enjoyed in Golden Atlantis are all being returned to those of us who are responsible enough to use them. During that Golden Era there was a multitude of tools available to the priesthood to keep their personal frequencies and that of their surrounding areas pure and clear. Homes, temples, land, water and food were kept at a sparkling fifth-dimensional vibration by the continual vigilance of the priests. Everyone benefited from this for a period of 1,500 years, until the Atlantis experiment devolved for the final time. Now, the frequency and collective consciousness of the lightworker team has risen to the point where the tools can be returned to us.

The high priests Voosloo and Thoth, along with Archangel Metatron, will install the Instant Sun directly into your solar plexus and then activate it for you for the first time. After that you will be expected to use this tool with the wisdom and responsibility of a walking master.

Once activated, the Instant Sun encompasses your energy field, burning away any frequencies that you wish to change or find undesirable. This can include cords and attachments, other people's energies and karma, energetic implants, entities or anything else functioning from a source of polarity.

Once you feel clear, the Instant Sun can then be collapsed upon command and will shrink to a tiny nucleus containing the energies that you have now removed. Archangel Uriel and the unicorns will then transmute the dense energy into higher light.

Whilst the Instant Sun is collapsing, you can ask it to draw in the fresh higher energy that you now wish to have in your fields. You must be very clear about the new that you wish to attract, as thoughts manifest very quickly now.

Here is an example of how it works. Imagine you have a shed in your garden that is full of cobwebs and old junk. When you call in the Instant Sun, it forms a ball of light over the shed and Voosloo, Thoth and Archangel Metatron activate it. The frequency becomes so high that all the dirt is swept up into a tiny ball, then illuminated and transmuted by Archangel Uriel and the unicorns into pure light. Then you fill the shed with the shiny new tools that you require.

This is a visualization to receive the Instant Sun and to learn how to use it for yourself:

Visualization to Receive the Instant Sun

1. Prepare a space where you can be relaxed and undisturbed. Light a candle if you can.

2. Sit quietly and breathe comfortably with the intention of receiving and working with the Instant Sun.

3. Ground yourself by visualizing roots going from your feet deep into the Earth.

4. Ask Archangel Michael to place his deep blue cloak of protection around you.

5. Visualize your 12-chakra system lighting up and activating at a fifth-dimensional frequency:

   your Stellar Gateway, glowing bright gold

   your soul star, glowing bright magenta

   your causal chakra, shining like the Moon

   your crown, glowing crystal gold

   your third eye, crystal clear but shining with a clear emerald light

   your throat, royal blue

   your heart, pure white with soft pink touches

   your solar plexus, pure gold

   your navel, radiant orange

   your sacral, the softest pink

   your base, shining, swirling platinum

   your cobalt grey Earth Star

6. As they all glow with your mastery and magnificence, intend them to become a unified column of light stretching up to the core of Helios, the Great Central Sun, and down to be anchored into the core of Hollow Earth. Visualize this.

7. Invoke the presence of the great Lord Voosloo and the mighty Thoth. Sense them join you as you sit quietly radiating your ascended frequency.

8. Say, either aloud or mentally:

   'I now gratefully accept my gift of the Instant Sun.'

9. Lord Voosloo now places a bright golden ball in your solar plexus chakra, gently smoothing the energy into place. Feel it vibrating and glowing.

10. Your Instant Sun is now ready to be activated. Say aloud or mentally:

    'Instant Sun, activate.'

11. From your solar plexus a bright ball of Sun energy spreads around your body, aura and fields. You are glowing with powerful light.

12. Feel it burning away any emotions, energies, cords and attachments or anything else that you wish to replace with a higher light.

13. Feel the new, higher, energy rushing in to replace the old.

14. The Instant Sun is now in place around your energy fields. Expand it as far as you wish.

Afterword

We very much hope you have enjoyed reading *The Archangel Guide to Ascension: 55 Steps to the Light*.

The words contained in the pages are designed to affect the conscious and subconscious mind and will continue to have an illuminating effect upon you long after the text has been read.

Between the point of writing and the time of reading, the energies of our planet will have changed again.

Every new day brings an increase in frequency, an opportunity for transformation and a reshaping of the reality around us.

Our world is set to have shifted fully into a fifth-dimensional template by the year 2032 and by then the geometric set-up of the supporting energies will have changed again. Planet Earth will be a very different place to live on, and you, the reader, will be fully on your path to walking mastery.

We wish you love, laughter, abundance and light on your transformational journey.

Life here is for learning and expansion, creating your own reality and remembering who you really are.

Use the tools and information within this book to boost this light within yourself and pass this to others, no matter where they may be along their pathway.

Love and many blessings,

Diana Cooper and Tim Whild

ABOUT THE AUTHORS

Wayne Lawes

Diana Cooper received an angel visitation during a time of personal crisis. She is now well known for her work with angels, Orbs, Atlantis, unicorns, ascension and the transition to the new Golden Age. Through her guides and angels she enables people to access their spiritual gifts and psychic potential, and also connects them to their own angels, guides, Masters and unicorns.

Diana is the founder of The Diana Cooper Foundation, a not-for-profit organization that offers certificated spiritual teaching courses throughout the world. She is also the bestselling author of 25 books, which have been published in 27 languages.

Peter Whild

Tim Whild is an ascension and Lightbody expert, who has been working closely with the evolvement of Earth for most of his life.

Tim was a High Priest in the eras of Atlantis and Ancient Egypt, and is using his collective memories to bring through the spiritual gifts and information stored in those times. His current work with ancient Atlantean technologies is already helping those on a spiritual path around the world.

Tim runs workshops and Skype sessions, and writes a regular blog for his co-author, Diana Cooper. This is his first book to be published in the field of esoterica.

www.dianacooper.com
www.timwhild.com

CPSIA information can be obtained
at www.ICGtesting.com
Printed in the USA
FSOW01n0316170415
6477FS